PROGRAMMED VOCABULARY

Third Edition

PROGRAMMED

PRENTICE-HALL, Inc., Englewood Cliffs, New Jersey 07632

VOCABULARY

the CPD approach

JAMES I. BROWN
Professor of Rhetoric
University of Minnesota

Library of Congress Cataloging in Publication Data

BROWN, JAMES ISAAC, 1908–
  Programmed vocabulary.

  1. Vocabulary—Programmed instruction. I. Title.
PE1449.B725 1980   428′.1′077   79-25186
ISBN 0-13-729707-6

PROGRAMMED VOCABULARY
the CPD approach
third edition
JAMES I. BROWN

Printed in the United States of America

10 9 8 7 6 5 4 3 2 1

Editorial/production supervision by Wendy Terryberry and Douglas Kubach
Interior design by Lee Cohen
Cover design by Saiki & Sprung Design
Manufacturing buyer: Harry P. Baisley

PRENTICE-HALL INTERNATIONAL, INC., London
PRENTICE-HALL OF AUSTRALIA PTY. LIMITED, Sydney
PRENTICE-HALL OF CANADA, LTD., Toronto
PRENTICE-HALL OF INDIA PRIVATE LIMITED, New Delhi
PRENTICE HALL OF JAPAN, INC., Tokyo
PRENTICE-HALL OF SOUTHEAST ASIA PTE. LTD., Singapore
WHITEHALL BOOKS LIMITED, WELLINGTON, New Zealand

To my wife
who has helped this book from first idea
to final form

CONTENTS

PART THREE

ROOTS

PART FOUR

SUFFIXES

PART FIVE

PREFACE

PROGRAMMED VOCABULARY brings you a particularly useful approach to vocabulary development. Its usefulness grows out of four distinctive characteristics.

Programmed Form

First, it's in programmed form. One educator went so far as to call programmed instruction the greatest forward step in education since the invention of movable type back in the eleventh century.

That enthusiasm is understandable. Just take a closer look at conventional, non-programmed books. With them it's all too easy to slip into a passive or semi-passive state as you read—to read without really reading. To be sure, your eyes travel down the pages. But when you've finished a page, section or chapter, you realize that your attention has wandered. Portions of the book are a complete blank. That's why the programmed format is so useful. It doesn't permit "passive" reading. It demands your active response every step of the way. Obviously, fifteen minutes of active, concentrated learning is far better than hours of desultory study.

Much the same thing can be noticed when you're called on in class. Your attention rises to top pitch. Every teacher has watched students transformed in an instant from passive listeners to active, alert responders in that situation. In a sense, programmed instruction capitalizes on this human characteristic. It's like having a private tutor by your side, asking a series of pointed questions to keep your attention and interest high. In short, the programmed form insures a more *active* participation.

Furthermore, programming capitalizes on the principle of "errorless learning." Each step is so closely related to the preceding one that with reasonable concentration, mistakes are reduced to a minimum. If you do happen to make a mistake, it is corrected immediately before it becomes established and has to be unlearned.

The programmed form also capitalizes on what psychologists call *reinforcement*, thought by some to be the most important factor of all in learning. It's that immediate check or reinforcement of the right answer that fixes it so firmly in your mind. The more often this occurs and the sooner it follows your writing of a response, the better you learn.

Economy of Learning

Second, this book is designed to teach much through little. Essentially there are two ways of learning most things: individually, bit by bit, or collectively, all at once. As an example, take a certain list of 3,000 words which you must learn to spell. You can learn to spell all 3,000 of them, one by one—a monumental task. Or—you can accomplish the same goal by learning *one* single principle or rule, which governs the spelling of all 3,000.

In this text the numbered steps or frames, as they are called, are phrased so as to bring out such underlying principles or rules. Here is a frame drawn from the text which illustrates how this works. Notice how you're led past the individual case to think in terms of an underlying principle

When you add pre- to *empt* to make preempt, you keep both *e*'s.

Similarly, when you add *inter-* to racial you should spell the resulting combination _____. (*interracial*)

As you can see, that one frame should help you with hundreds of similar combinations, even such tricky ones as *sub + basement, news + stand, re + echo, dis + service* and the like. In this way you learn how to spell words not even mentioned. That's what we mean by teaching much through little.

In exactly the same way, why not learn one word part so as to help you with the meanings of up to a thousand additional words— words not even mentioned. After all, building a vocabulary one word at a time is painfully slow. That's why the emphasis here is on learning much through little. This book may actually do more to improve your vocabulary than a conventional book four or five times its size.

Such an approach demands a special shortcut — the fourteen most important words in the English language for speeding your vocabulary development. Leonard A. Stevens, in a *Coronet* article called them "The 14 Words That Make All the Difference." That's because they contain the twenty most important prefixes and the fourteen most important roots. They're called most important because their word parts are found in *over 14,000 words* of collegiate dictionary size or close to 100,000 words from the big unabridged dictionary. That means that each single word provides you with a key to the meanings of at least 1,000 words. Those are the select few which are studied in depth in this text.

But word mastery depends also on memory. All too often students say, "I just can't remember those prefix and root meanings." In a sense, forget one and you've forgotten a thousand. What you need is another principle to help — the principle of mnemonics. Suppose, for example, you can't remember what the prefix *hypo-* means. Put mnemonics to work. The following frame suggests how to do it.

> To remember that *hypo-* means "under," think where the doctor puts the
> ____dermic needle when you get a shot.

Visualize that gleaming, glistening hypodermic needle poised above your arm — all ready to be pushed *under* your skin. Let painful experience provide you with an indelible reminder that *hypo-* means "under." Of course you are the one who must actively make associations of that kind. They don't make themselves. Once vividly made, however, your forgetting problems are over.

Be sure to take full advantage of *everything* in a frame. For ex-example, did you wonder what *dermic* meant? If you did, you probably decided it meant "skin." That would open the way to understanding such technical words as *dermatology, dermatogen, dermatone, dermiti-tis,* and *dermatophytosis,* which is just a fancy way of saying athlete's foot.

Assimilation is still another principle of major importance in understanding word changes. The word *assimilation* both names and illustrates the process or principle. Frame after frame will bring you a sharpened awareness of how assimilation works.

For example, what do the following words have in common: *ascend, accept, aggregate, ally, annex, append, arrive, assimilate* and *attract?* If you haven't studied this text, you'll probably say, "They all begin with *a.*" Actually, all of them show the effects of assimilation, all containing forms of one single prefix, the prefix *ad-,* in its many assimilative disguises. See how the third letter in each word changes or assimilates the final *d* in *ad-.*

Approximately 60 to 70 percent of all assimilative changes can be easily spotted by noting the sign of the doubled initial consonant. This principle of identification is reinforced by such frames as this:

To aid in spotting assimilative changes, remember *oppress, occlude,* and *offer.* In all three words the second and ___ letters are identical.

In addition to the 14-word shortcut, mnemonics, and assimilation, other less broadly applicable principles are also stressed to expedite more rapid progress. As a final step, you will be introduced to a formula specifically designed to help you deal more effectively with hundreds of prefix root and suffix elements not covered in these pages — true economy of learning.

The CPD Formula

Here is the third major characteristic. What does *napl* mean? You don't know? No wonder. Those four letters are not properly organized. To make them meaningful, re-arrange them into the word *plan.*

The right format (programmed instruction) and the right emphasis (much through little) are both important, but you still need something more — the right plan. For when you fail to plan, you're actually planning to fail.

The CPD Formula or plan should provide an ideal structuring for your vocabulary-building efforts. Here's the rationale.

C-for Context. When students in an Efficient Reading class were asked what they should do when they came across an unfamiliar word, there was little disagreement. Eighty-four percent said, "Look it up in the dictionary." Yet, to speed your vocabulary development, that's probably the very worst advice you can follow.

To see why, try the following two-item vocabulary test.

1. *extenuate* a) lessen, b) make less serious, c) belittle, **1.** _____
d) make thin, e) reduce the strength of.

2. *loggerhead* a) a turtle, b) an iron tool, c) a post on **2.** _____
a whaleboat, d) a blockhead, e) a carnivorous bird.

Did you get both items right? You can be absolutely certain you did — *no matter which choices you made.* All five choices are *correct* — correct dictionary definitions of the word in question.

Most words have more than one meaning. For the common word *fast,* for example, the dictionary lists not one but twenty-one separate definitions. Some are poles apart, such as "swift moving" and "firmly fastened," as in the sentence, "The fast horse was tied fast." Actually the 500 most common words in the English language have a total of 14,070 separate meanings — an average of 28 per word. That's why it's almost pointless to ask what any given word means: It all depends — it depends on context, on the way the word is used. In short, unless the word has only one meaning, you must rely on context, not the dictionary, for its exact meaning. That's why the formula begins with context.

Furthermore, people vary widely in their ability to use contextual clues. In one class, for example, a difficult vocabulary test was given, first without contexts, next with contexts. Two students made identical scores of thirty each without context. The second time through, with context, one moved up to ninety, the other up to only forty. As suggested by this example, some have developed remarkable skill in using contextual clues; others haven't as yet.

P-for Parts.   Now while context is a strong determiner of meaning it is not always sufficiently complete. That brings us to the need for word parts. Take the sentence, "The student had a predilection for novels." That meager context doesn't really tell you much about what *predilection* means — whether the student likes novels or dislikes them.

So — look for useful word parts. Is there a prefix, root, or suffix that will help? You may not know what *predilection* means, but you probably do know that *pre-* means "before." And that added information is quite helpful. Novels apparently come "before" other types of reading in that student's list of likings. Roots and suffixes help in the same way to uncover word meanings.

D-for Dictionary.   Finally, to get the active involvement needed for maximum progress, consult the dictionary *last* — after you've tried both context and word parts to lead you to a tentative definition of word meaning. Then, and only then, should you turn to the dictionary. By that time you're actively involved. You have stuck your neck out. You say, "From context and word part evidence, I think *predilection* probably means "preference,' and the sentence probably means the student had a preference for novels."

Notice how this last step heightens your interest in the word in question. Are you right or wrong in your conclusion? You reach for the dictionary to find out. How well did you use the available clues? Sure enough. The actual dictionary definition for *predilection* is "preference." Savor that strong feeling of satisfaction in being right. Never underestimate the value of success as a motivational force.

But what if you're wrong? In that case, you have the best of opportunities to see exactly why and where you got off the track, which means you should do much better next time.

So much for the way the CPD Formula operates. You can see that if you go to the dictionary first, you short circuit the very mental process needed to hasten your vocabulary development. Just as a short circuit wastes electricity, so reaching for the dictionary first wastes brain power. Such a move tends to dissipate instead of cultivate the intellectual curiosity which adds dynamic power to your efforts. In brief, the CPD plan provides a balanced, dynamic approach for this book.

Special Test Types

The fourth and last characteristic of this book is its use of special types of vocabulary test items—*opposites, analogies* and *completions.* These have a double usefulness. First, they serve an ideal review function, demanding as they do a particularly thoughtful consideration of words and word parts. Second, they prepare you to cope more effectively with any such tests as the Scholastic Aptitude Test (SAT), Miller Analogy Test, Civil Service Tests, College Boards, Scholarship Tests and Graduate Record Examinations, where these types of test items are typically found. Employers in general are also turning more and more frequently to vocabulary-type tests as aids in screening and selecting personnel. Practice in dealing with such items takes on, therefore, a heightened practical advantage.

Mini-reviews, built around mnemonic aids, are also used. They provide a quick way to do three things: 1) given a word part, to review its meaning, 2) given a meaning, to review the word part contributing that meaning and 3) given a mnemonic association, to move you more easily toward both meaning and word part. Mini-reviews mean maxi-gains.

So much for the four essential characteristics of this book--**1)** The Programmed Format, **2)** Economy of Learning, **3)** The Dynamic CPD Plan, and **4)** Special Test Types.

Now you're ready for the first step—*Diagnosis.*

In preparing this third edition of **Programmed Vocabulary,** I am particularly indebted to the following reviewers for their perceptive and helpful suggestions: Marvyl Doyle of El Camino College, Leonore Ganschow of Northern Kentucky University and William F. Woods of Wichita State University. Their sharing of experience helped immeasurably in the preparing of this edition. I should like also to express appreciation to my colleague, J. Michael Bennett, who, from his use of the earlier edition here at Minnesota, contributed important insights.

Particular thanks should also go to my wife, Ruth, who worked through each page of the manuscript, serving as editor and encourager in its several stages. Her training and experience as a certified SLBO tutor added an important vantage point. Finally, to Kathleen M. Sands, Associate English Editor for Prentice-Hall, Inc., special thanks for her contribution in arranging for review evaluations and providing reactions, support and encouragement to expedite progress.

St. Paul, Minnesota   **J. I. B.**

PROGRAMMED VOCABULARY

PART ONE

CPD DIAGNOSIS

The following diagnostic test will answer three key questions:

I. *CONTEXT:* How well do you use the context to get word meanings?

II. *PARTS:* How well do you use word parts – prefixes, roots, and suffixes – to get word meanings?
A. Memorization ┐
B. Identification │ (Four-part in-depth
C. Application │ exploration)
D. Generalization ┘
Parts Score Total

III. *DICTIONARY:* How well do you use the dictionary to get accurate information about words and word parts?

A word of warning: The following tests are all quite difficult. That's so you can see progress more clearly. After all, if you score 100 percent to begin with, what further progress can you possibly see? Any frustration you feel now – and you'll probably feel far too much – should be more than compensated for by your greatly improved performance when you finish this text, after an estimated twelve to sixteen hours of work. In a sense, the lower your scores now, the better. The more room you have for improvement, the more important this book, and the greater its challenge.

Do the following tests without looking up any of the answers. You want to know which of these three areas needs most attention – which area you should concentrate on for maximum improvement.

Do not check any answers until you have finished the entire test.

I. Context Test

When you meet a strange word, how well do you use contextual clues to get its meaning? Let's find out. We'll use a two-step procedure. First you'll take a vocabulary test—ten items without any context to help. Then you'll take the same test, but this time you'll have contexts to use.

Now take the following ten-item vocabulary test, putting your answers in the column headed A. It's intended to be so difficult you may not get even one right, for if you already know the words, you don't need contextual help. And the important thing here is to find out how well you use context. So—go right ahead. Answer *all* ten items. Then continue as directed below.

	A	*B*
1. *Refectory* means (1) kitchen; (2) mirror; (3) dining room; (4) washroom; (5) living room. **1.** ____ ____		
2. *Preferment* means (1) burial; (2) precedent; (3) sickness; (4) advancement; (5) choice. **2.** ____ ____		
3. *Canaille* means (1) mob; (2) dog hospital; (3) visitors; (4) soldiers; (5) students. **3.** ____ ____		
4. *Glabrous* means (1) large; 2) bald; (3) sharp; (4) icy; (5) glamorous. **4.** ____ ____		
5. *Capriole* means (1) whim; (2) leap; (3) trot; (4) flourish; (5) rest. **5.** ____ ____		
6. *Halcyon* means (1) brilliant; (2) memorable; (3) clear; (4) tranquil; (5) ecstatic. **6.** ____ ____		
7. *Mephitic* means (1) intoxicating; (2) soothing; (3) harmful; (4) methodical; (5) healthful. **7.** ____ ____		
8. *Epergne* means (1) centerpiece; (2) antique; (3) sword; (4) classical poem; (5) salad. **8.** ____ ____		
9. *Abecedarian* means (1) expert; (2) grammarian; (3) stranger; (4) beginner; (5) teacher. **9.** ____ ____		
10. *Mawkish* means (1) fumbling; (2) sickening; (3) awkward; (4) droll; (5) colorful. **10.** ____ ____		

Now for the second step. Here are sentence contexts for each of the above ten words. Study each; then go back to the test item and enter the answer that seems to fit the context best. Use column B for this second set of answers. Don't change any answers in column A. Sometimes, of course, you may have the same answer in both columns.

1. Sometimes the helper worked inside, sweeping crumbs off the refectory floor from around the tables.
2. If you want preferment, work so hard you'll stand out above all others.
3. The unruly, shouting canaille burst into the palace, smashing down the doors.
4. As he walked, his glabrous head reflected the street lights.
5. The spectators watched the horse execute a perfectly timed capriole.
6. Their restful vacations in the mountain solitudes brought them halcyon days.
7. A stupifying mephitic gas came pouring out of a vent into the crowded room, leading to serious consequences.
8. As they entered the dining room, they saw the beautiful epergne on the table.
9. Well, you've had years of skiing experience. I'm just an abecedarian.
10. The movie was so mawkish, we left in the middle — just couldn't stand any more!

Now you should have two complete sets of answers. Score them as directed below *after* you have completed this entire three-part diagnostic test.

Give yourself ten for each one right, scoring each set separately. If you made perfect use of context, you will score 100 in column B. The difference between your scores with and without context indicates how well you use contextual clues.

Your score for this part, therefore, is your column B score *minus* your column A score. If, however, your score in column A is 50 or more, multiply your column B minus column A score *by two* to get your context score.

II. Parts Test

II A: MEMORIZATION

To measure your skill in using word parts, you need four tests, not one, for skillful use of word parts depends on four separate insights or skills. As with your fingerprints, your score on these subtests will carry your individual mark. You may do very well in one area, very poorly in another. But, when you have finished all four subtests, you will know exactly where to concentrate your attention to get the best results. You will know exactly what strengths to build on and what weaknesses to correct.

This first subtest of word parts measures your rote knowledge of the common meanings of ten prefixes and ten roots, an indication of your awareness of all such elements.

Again, this is a difficult test. You will probably have to guess frequently. Be sure to get an answer down for each item, even if you are not sure of its meaning. Obviously if you do not know what a given prefix or root means, you cannot use it as a shortcut. And since each element helps you with close to a thousand words, you can hardly afford not to know and use them as shortcuts to word meaning.

To broaden the measure of your prefix and root knowledge, the following word-part tests contain some prefixes and roots not included in the fourteen words to be studied in depth. This is so that when you finish the text you can see more clearly what progress you've made. If you develop superior ability, you'll be able to deal accurately with elements studied in depth as well as with many others.

NAME _____

Test II A

MEMORIZATION

1. *Re-* means (1) together; (2) upon; (3) back or again; (4) behind; 5) out of.

1. _____

2. *Mono-* means (1) some; (2) now; (3) still; (4) alone; (5) almost.

2. _____

3. *Sub-* means (1) beside; (2) apart from; (3) out; (4) under; (5) in front of.

3. _____

4. *Mis-* means (1) wrong; (2) cruel; (3) different; (4) late; (5) old.

4. _____

5. *Com-* means (1) every; (2) through; (3) after; (4) together; (5) in.

5. _____

6. *Ad-* means (1) for; (2) with; (3) to or toward; (4) from; (5) only or without.

6. _____

7. *Inter-* means (1) inside; (2) between; (3) near; (4) forward; (5) among.

7. _____

8. *Ab-* means (1) bad; (2) take out; (3) below; (4) away from; (5) not.

8. _____

9. *Pro-* means (1) together with; (2) to go; (3) behind; (4) forward; (5) outside.

9. _____

10. *Para-* means (1) more; (2) beginning; (3) present; (4) past; (5) beside.

10. _____

11. *Scribere* means (1) write; (2) stretch; (3) speak; (4) scratch; (5) frighten.

11. _____

12. *Videre* means (1) eat; (2) catch; (3) value; (4) shake; (5) see.

12. _____

13. *Ferre* means (1) bear or carry; (2) float; (3) rust; (4) put or place; (5) enter.

13. _____

14. *Facere* means (1) put; (2) fear; (3) make; (4) fill; (5) lead.

14. _____

15. *Sequi* means (1) decorate; (2) quiet; (3) cure; (4) follow; (5) preach.

15. _____

16. *Logos* (legein) means (1) speech or science; (2) locate or find; (3) raise; (4) limit; (5) leave.

16. _____

17. *Vertere* means (1) turn; (2) speak; (3) inform; (4) watch; (5) voyage.

17. _____

18. *Mittere* means (1) send; (2) catch; (3) release; (4) tire; (5) earn.

18. _____

19. *Sedere* means (1) cut off; (2) speak; (3) sit; (4) select; (5) satisfy.

19. _____

20. *Claudere* means (1) climb; (2) divide; (3) clean; (4) eliminate; (5) shut.

20. _____

II B: IDENTIFICATION

This second subtest of word parts measures your ability to identify prefixes and roots as they normally appear in words. You must know, for example, that every word beginning with *pre* does not contain the prefix *pre-*. The prefix *pre-* is in *prefer* but not in *pretzel*. The prefix *ad-* is in *admit* but not in *adynamic*. In short, if a given word begins with the exact letters of any prefix, it still may or may not contain that prefix.

Root elements pose the same kind of problem. The roots *mitt* and *miss* may look quite different, yet the English words *admitting* and *admission* suggest that they are but different forms of the same root.

Obviously, to take full advantage of prefixes and roots as shortcuts you must be able to make such distinctions. This subtest provides a measure of that ability. The remainder of the book provides help so that you become skilled in making those distinctions.

Don't worry about mistakes. If you have no trouble with this test, you know the book is too elementary for you. Only when you try something beyond present mastery do you grow. An easy book is antigrowth. You want your work to bring real improvement.

NAME _____

Test II B

IDENTIFICATION

1. *Monopoly* contains a form of (1) *homo-;* (2) *multi-;* (3) *non-;* (4) *mono-;* (5) none of the preceding prefixes.

    1. _____

2. *Correlation* contains a form of (1) *contra-;* (2) *circum-;* (3) *re-;* (4) *ab-;* (5) none of the preceding prefixes.

    2. _____

3. *Suppress* contains a form of (1) *super-;* (2) *supra-;* (3) *pre-;* (4) *sub;* (5) none of the preceding prefixes.

    3. _____

4. *Misnomer* contains a form of (1) *iso-;* (2) *mid-;* (3) *mini-;* (4) *mis-;* (5) none of the preceding prefixes.

    4. _____

5. Collaborate contains a form of (1) *com-;* (2) *counter-;* (3) *contra-;* (4) *ab-;* (5) none of the preceding prefixes.

    5. _____

6. *Adder* contains a form of (1) *ana-;* (2) *ad-;* (3) *amphi-;* (4) *de-;* (5) none of the preceding prefixes.

    6. _____

7. *Intercept* contains a form of (1) *in-;* (2) *intro-;* (3) *ex-;* (4) *inter-;* (5) none of the preceding prefixes.

    7. _____

8. *Aversion* contains a form of (1) *ab-;* (2) *aut-;* (3) *ana-;* (4) *ex-;* (5) none of the preceding prefixes.

    8. _____

9. *Reproduce* contains a form of (1) *retro-;* (2) *pro-;* (3) *ob-;* (4) *post;* (5) none of the preceding prefixes.

    9. _____

10. *Parallel* contains a form of (1) *pan-;* (2) *pyro-;* (3) *para-;* (4) *ad-;* (5) none of the preceding prefixes.

    10. _____

11. The word *nondescript* contains a form of (1) *densus;* (2) *crescere;* (3) *stringere;* (4) *ducere;* (5) none of the preceding roots.

11. _____

12. *Video* contains a form of (1) *videre;* (2) *vincere;* (3) *volvere;* (4) *verus;* (5) none of the preceding roots.

12. _____

13. *Feature* contains a form of (1) *ferre;* (2) *forma;* (3) *fundere;* (4) *fluere;* (5) none of the preceding roots.

13. _____

14. *Factory* contains a form of (1) *actus;* (2) *facere;* (3) *capere;* (4) *agere;* (5) none of the preceding roots.

14. _____

15. *Sequel* contains a form of (1) *quaerere;* (2) *sequi;* (3) *equitare;* (4) *sentire;* (5) none of the preceding roots.

15. _____

16. *Sociology* contains a form of (1) *senex;* (2) *logos;* (3) *ludere;* (4) *cito;* (5) none of the preceding roots.

16. _____

17. *Versatile* contains a form of (1) *vertere;* (2) *satiare;* (3) *venire;* (4) *jacere;* (5) none of the preceding roots.

17. _____

18. *Admission* contains a form of (1) *addere;* (2) *dicere;* (3) *mutare;* (4) *mittere;* (5) none of the preceding roots.

18. _____

19. *Sediment* probably contains a form of (1) *sedere;* (2) *sentire;* (3) *dicere;* (4) *edere;* (5) none of the preceding roots.

19. _____

20. *Include* probably contains a form of (1) *caput;* (2) *clinare;* (3) *ludere;* (4) *claudere;* (5) none of the preceding roots.

20. _____

II C: APPLICATION

This third subtest measures the important payoff step. You may know what a prefix or root means (memorization) and may be able to identify the element correctly in a word (identification), but how well can you apply that information to unlock word meanings? This subtest provides a measure of your skill in application. You may score perfectly in the first two tests but still have difficulty here. These difficult words all have prefixes or roots which should be of help—*if* you have developed sufficient skill in putting them to use.

NAME _____

Test II C

APPLICATION

1. *Relumed* means   (1) lighted again; (2) torn into bits; (3) filled up; (4) brightened; (5) lined up.

1. _____

2. *Monostich* means   (1) headache; (2) catalog; (3) radio; (4) line of poetry; (5) lining.

2. _____

3. *Sublunary* means   (1) luminous; (2) oval; (3) solar; (4) unreasoning; (5) earthly.

3. _____

4. *Miscreant* means   (1) dramatist; (2) executive; (3) speaker; (4) heretic; (5) warrior.

4. _____

5. *Compendium* means   (1) summary; (2) pencil; (3) pretense; (4) extension; (5) discarding.

5. _____

6. *Adminicular* means   (1) retiring; (2) small; (3) broken down; (4) strange; (5) helping.

6. _____

7. *Interlope* means   (1) elude; (2) chase; (3) intrude; (4) modify; (5) limp.

7. _____

8. *Aberrant* means   (1) inclusive; (2) relevant; (3) tired; (4) deviating; (5) sane.

8. _____

9. *Prolocutor* means   (1) spouse; (2) spokesman; (3) orator; (4) plan; (5) typist.

9. _____

10. *Paradigm* means   (1) falsehood; (2) model; (3) exception; (4) eruption; (5) problem.

10. _____

11. *Escritoire* means   (1) writing desk; (2) raven; (3) drinking fountain; (4) paper; (5) bank.

11. _____

12. *Vis-à-vis* means (1) back to back; (2) new; (3) alike; (4) face to face; (5) side by side.

12. _____

13. *Feracious* means (1) fierce; (2) gentle; (3) solid; (4) barren; (5) fruitful.

13. _____

14. *Facile* means (1) skillful; (2) struggling; (3) conservative; (4) beginning; (5) deserving.

14. _____

15. *Sequela* means (1) remedy; (2) following thing; (3) quiz; (4) struggle; (5) big tree.

15. _____

16. *Logogriph* means (1) wooden peg; (2) gun; (3) container; (4) word puzzle; (5) handle.

16. _____

17. *Divert* means (1) remove; (2) turn aside; (3) make ready; (4) display; (5) remain.

17. _____

18. *Missive* means (1) mask; (2) message; (3) star; (4) question; (5) weapon.

18. _____

19. *Sedate* means (1) worldly; (2) composed; (3) religious; (4) secretive; (5) slovenly.

19. _____

20. *Claustral* means (1) fatty; (2) harmful; (3) confined; (4) clear; (5) stormy.

20. _____

II D: GENERALIZATION

Every day you must rely on generalizations about people and things. When you taste three green, hard apples and discover all of them are sour, you generalize that *all* green, hard apples are sour. Obviously, generalizing is a very useful ability to cultivate.

If you can sharpen your ability to generalize accurately about words and word parts, you can then make quantum leaps in your vocabulary development. This fourth and last subtest of word parts attempts to measure how accurately you now generalize. Again, try each item. Do not leave any answer spaces blank.

NAME _____

Test II D

GENERALIZATION

1. The prefix *dis-* is not in   (1) *displease;* (2) *indif-ferent;* (3) *diffuse;* (4) *distract;* (5) *dish.*   1. _____

2. The prefix *de-* is not in   (1) *defer;* (2) *debar;* (3) *condescend;* (4) *decrease;* (5) *death.*   2. _____

3. Which of the following prefixes is most likely to change in form?   (1) *hyper-;* (2) *pre-;* (3) *mono-;* (4) *com-;* (5) *de-.*   3. _____

4. The prefix *ex-* is usually spelled *ef-* before a root beginning with   (1) *f,* (2) *g;* (3) *s;* (4) *m;* (5) *c.*   4. _____

5. If there were a prefix *rib-* to be combined with *port,* the probable form would be   (1) *ripport;* (2) *rib-port;* (3) *riport;* (4) *ribbort;* (5) *ribort.*   5. _____

6. The most frequent variations in prefix form are found with the prefixes ending in   (1) a vowel; (2) a consonant; (3) a diphthong; (4) a double vowel; (5) an m.   6. _____

7. In English words, the *-ere* or *-are* of many Latin roots is normally   (1) retained; (2) changed to *-er;* (3) changed to *-or;* (4) changed to *-re;* (5) dropped.   7. _____

8. If you combined the imaginary prefix *ud-* with *nex,* the probable resulting form would be   (1) *unnex;* (2) *udnex;* (3) *uddex;* (4) *unex;* (5) *udex.*   8. _____

9. Variations in original classical root elements coming over into English usually occur in what part? (1) no particular part; (2) the last part; (3) the middle part; (4) the first part.   9. _____

10. English words derived from classical sources make up about how much of our language?   (1) 20%; (2) 30%; (3) 40%; (4) 50%; (5) 60%.

10. _____

11. The Latin word *fluo,* found in *fluid* and *flux,* probably means   (1) force; (2) year; (3) flow; (4) harden; (5) file.

11. _____

12. *Omni-,* found in *omnibus, omnipresent,* and *omniverous,* probably means   (1) solid; (2) free; (3) single; (4) old; (5) all.

12. _____

13. *Fundo,* found in *funnel* and *refund,* probably means (1) shape; (2) bind; (3) pour; (4) pay; (5) fall.

13. _____

14. *Ardeo,* found in *ardor* and *arson,* probably means (1) burn; (2) tree; (3) love; (4) cruel; (5) equal.

14. _____

15. *Meta-,* found in *metamorphosis* and *metabolism* probably means   (1) fixed; (2) altered; (3) spoken; (4) outlined; (5) discovered.

15. _____

16. *Valeo,* found in *valor,* and *invalid,* probably means (1) level; (2) weak; (3) old; (4) strong; (5) colorful.

16. _____

17. *Dies,* found in *diary* and *diurnal,* probably means (1) book; (2) day; (3) pen; (4) year; (5) skill.

17. _____

18. *Aristos,* found in *aristocrat,* probably means   (1) best; (2) ancient; (3) vain; (4) recent; (5) artistic.

18. _____

19. After thinking of some words beginning with *mega-,* which meaning seems best for that word part?   (1) limited; (2) sure; (3) middling; (4) powerful; (5) artificial.

19. _____

20. After thinking of some words probably derived from from *pendeo,* which meaning seems best?   (1) hang; (2) judge; (3) pierce; (4) exchange; (5) feel (Did you think of *pend*ant or *pend*ulum?)

20. _____

III. Dictionary Test

Academically speaking, your best friend is your dictionary. It plays a key role in the CPD approach, fusing context and parts together into a dynamic vocabulary-building whole. But dictionaries crowd so much into small space that you need to develop special skills to get accurate information.

How accurately can you now use this highly specialized aid? Take this test to find out. Use the dictionary entries below to answer the twenty questions. All questions, however, are not answered in these entries. So if the information is not there, enter a dash or the phrase, "no information" in the answer space and move on to the next item.

☆**ad**[1] (ad) *n.* [Colloq.] an advertisement

ad[2] (ad) *n. Tennis* advantage (sense 4): said of the first point scored after deuce — ad in server's advantage — ad out receiver's advantage

ad- ad, əd, id) [L. *ad-*, to, at, toward; akin to AT] *a prefix meaning variously* motion toward, addition to, nearness to [*admit; adjoin; adrenal*]: assimilated in words of Latin origin to *ac-* before *c* or *q*, *af-* before *f*, *ag-* before *g*, *al-* before *l*, *an-* before *n*, *ap-* before *p*, *ar-* before *r*, *as-* before *s*, *at-* before *t*, and *a-* before *sc*, *sp*, and *st:* many apparent English occurrences of this prefix are Latinizations, often erroneous, of French or even of English words: see ADVANCE, ADMIRAL, ACCURSED, ACKNOWLEDGE

-ad[1] (ad, əd, id) [Gr. *-as, -ad-*] *a suffix meaning* of or relating to, *used in forming:* 1. the names of collective numerals [*monad*] 2. the names of some poems [*Iliad*] 3. the names of some plants [*cycad*]

-ad[2] (ad) [L. *ad*, toward] *a suffix meaning* toward, in the direction of [*caudad*]

-ite[1] (it) [ME. < OFr. or L. or Gr.: OFr. *-ite* < L. *-ita, -ites* < Gr. *-ites*, fem. *-itis*] *a n.-forming suffix meaning:* 1. a native, inhabitant, or citizen of [*Brooklynite*] 2. a descendant from or offspring of [*Israelite*] 3. an adherent of, believer in, or members of [*laborite*] 4. a product, esp. a commercially manufactured one [*lucite, dynamite, vulcanite*] 5. a fossil [*ammonite*] 6. a part of a body or bodily organ [*somite*] 7. [Fr., arbitrary alteration of *-ate*, -ATE[2]] a salt or ester of an acid whose name ends in *-ous* [*nitrite, sulfite*] 8. a (specified) mineral or rock [*anthracite, dolomite*]

-ite[2] (it; *in some words*, it) [L. *-itus*, ending of some past participles] a suffix used variously to form adjectives, nouns, and verbs [*finite, favorite, unite*]

ness (nes) *n.* [ME. *nesse* < OE. *naes* & ON. *nes*, akin to OE. *nosu*, NOSE] a promontory; headland; now chiefly in place names [*Inverness*]

-ness (nis, nəs) [ME. *-nesse* < OE. *-nes(s)*, akin to G. *-niss*, Goth. *-nassus* [for *-assus*, with *n-* < end of the base of weak verbs ending in *-atjan*)] *a n.-forming suffix meaning* state, quality, or instance of being [*greatness,· sadness, togetherness*]

nice (nis) *adj.* nic′er, nic′est [ME., strange, lazy, foolish < OFr. *nice, nisce*, stupid, foolish < L. *nescius*, ignorant not knowing < *nescire*, to be ignorant < *ne-*, not (see NO¹) + *scire*, to know: see SCIENCE] 1. difficult to please; fastidious; refined 2. delicate; precise; discriminative; subtle [*a nice* distinction] 3. calling for great care, accuracy, tact, etc., as in handling or discrimination [*a nice* problem] 4. *a)* able to make fine or delicate distinctions; delicately skillful; finely discriminating *b)* minutely accurate, as an instrument 5. having high standards of conduct; scrupulous 6. *a generalized term of approval meaning variously: a)* agreeable; pleasant; delightful *b)* attractive; pretty *c)* courteous and considerate *d)* conforming to approved social standards; respectable *e)* in good taste *f)* good; excellent 7. [Obs.] *a)* ignorant; foolish *b)* wanton *c)* coy; shy—*adv.* well, pleasingly, attractively, etc.: variously regarded as substandard, dialectal, or colloquial—*SYN.* see DAINTY—nice and [Colloq.] altogether, in a pleasing way [likes his tea *nice and* hot]—nice′ly *adv.*—nice′ness *n.*

spec-ta-tor (spek′tatər, spek tat′-) *n* [L. < pp. of *spectare*, to behold: see SPECTACLE] a person who sees or watches something without taking an active part; onlooker

spec-ter (spek′tər) *n.* [Fr. *spectre* < L. *spectrum*, an appearance, apparition < *spectare*, to behold: see SPECTACLE] 1. a ghost; apparition 2. any object of fear or dread. Also, Brit. sp., spec′tre

Webster's New World Dictionary.

Dictionary Diagnostic Quiz

1. In the sentence, "Picking the most appropriate definition requires some nice distinctions on your part," which of the seven numbered definitions of *nice* is intended?

   1. Def. #_____

2. In the sentence, "That's a nice song you're singing," which numbered definition of *nice* is intended?

   2. Def. #_____

3. In the sentence, "This is a nice mess you've gotten us into," which numbered definition of *nice* is intended?

   3. Def. #_____

4. In the sentence, "They're so nice in their dining habits they wouldn't think of going on a picnic," which definition of *nice* is intended?

   4. Def. #_____

5. In the sentence, "You showed a nice regard for their feelings at that difficult time," which definition of *nice* is intended?

   5. Def. #_____

6. How many different entries are there for the prefix *ad*?

   6. _____

7. The prefix *ad* means what?

   7. _____

8. Can *ad* also be used as a suffix? (*Yes, no*, or *no information*)

   8. _____

9. Is *ad* also an abbreviation? (*Yes, no*, or *no information*)

   9. _____

10. If the prefix *ad* were added to the word *stringent*, how would the resulting word be spelled?

    10. _____

11. If the prefix *ad* were added to the word *leviate*, how would the resulting word be spelled?

    11. _____

12. *Nice* came originally from what language?

    12. _____

13. *Nice* is most closely related to what language?

13. _____

14. The Latin verb *spectare* means what?

14. _____

15. What dictionary entry gives added information about *spectare*?

15. _____

16. The Latin word *spectrum* means what?

16. _____

17. The Latin verb *scire* means what?

17. _____

18. How is *ness* used — as word, abbreviation, prefix, or suffix?

18. _____

19. How many different entries are there for *ite*?

19. _____

20. If you are bashful, you are in a state of bashful____?

20. _____

Now you have completed all parts of the diagnostic test. Check your answers by turning to the section beginning on page 254. Give yourself five for each correct answer, except for the context test, which you score differently. For that, you follow the special scoring instructions described after that test.

Enter your eight scores in the appropriate boxes below.

I	II					III	
Context	Word Parts					Dic-tionary	CPD
	II A	II B	II C	II D	II Total		Total
☐	☐	☐	☐	☐	☐	☐	☐

When you have completed this entire book, retake the CPD diagnostic test, using it this second time as a progress test. Cover your original answers for this second time. The scores will give you an excellent indication of the progress you have made and let you know if there are still areas that deserve further attention. After all, a vocabulary, like Rome, is not built in a day. You want to make certain you have developed the insights, skills, and interests that will insure continued growth. Use the boxes below for your end-of-the book recheck and compare your scores with your initial scores above.

I			II			III	
Context			Word Parts			Dic-tionary	CPD
	II A	II B	II C	II D	II Total	tionary	Total
☐	☐	☐	☐	☐	☐	☐	☐

SELF-INTERPRETING PROFILE

To put your test results into more meaningful form, transfer your scores for each part of the test from page 21, to the appropriate boxes at the top of page 22. Then draw a heavy line under the number below which corresponds with the number in the box at the top of each column. Connect the resulting lines to make your complete profile picture.

To get your percentile rank, look along the line in which your raw score is located to the column at the left of the page. For example, if your score on Test II A is 75, look at the percentile rank column opposite that number, which indicates the 60–62 percentile rank.

If your score in any of the columns is above the top dotted line, you are high in that area—among the top 25 percent. If any score is between the two dotted lines, you are average—among the middle 50 percent. If any score is below the bottom dotted line, you are low in that area—among the bottom 25 percent.

DIAGNOSIS

%-ile	I–C	IIA	IIB	IIC	IID	P Total	III–D	CPD Total
	☐	☐	☐	☐	☐	☐	☐	☐
99	90+			100		325+	85+	530+
96–98		95+	95+		100	315–320	80	510–520
93–95				95		300–310		500
90–92	80		90			295		490–495
87–89						285–290	75	485
84–86		90	85	90		275–280		
81–83					95	270		480
78–80						265		470–475
75–77	70	85		85		260		465
72–74						255	70	455–460
69–71		80	80			250		
66–68						240–245		450
63–65				80				
60–62		75			90	235		445
57–59						230		440

54–56						225		435
51–53			75	75	85		65	430
48–50	60	70				220		425
45–47						215		420
42–44				70	80	200–210		415
39–41								410
36–38				65		195	60	405
33–35		65	70		75			400
30–32						190		390–395
27–29				60		185		385
24–26	50	60	65		70	180		380
21–23								370–375
18–20				55		175		365
15–17		55	60	50		170	55	360
12–14	40				65	165		355
9–11	30	50		45		155–160	50	
6–8	20	40	55			135–150		335–345
3–5	10	35	50	40	60	110–130	45	325–330
0–2	0	30	45	25	55	70–105	40	255–315

INTERPRETING YOUR PROFILE

Now take a close look at your profile sheet. It should help you plan exactly how to manage your learning efforts to best advantage. How well did you score in each of the three areas tested?

Part I: Context. The dictionary may say *extinguish* means "put out," but you still shouldn't say, "I think I'll extinguish the cat and retire." And the dictionary may define *vicarious* as "substitute," but that doesn't mean you should say, "We had a vicarious teacher today," even if you did have a substitute.

The context, not the dictionary, is needed for all such situations. Developing skilled use of contextual clues is a top priority. The lower your score in this first part of the test, the more carefully you should work through each frame, noting any and every clue possible before arriving at an answer. By so doing, you will take the very steps needed to improve your contextual skills. As you do, remember that vocabulary in context—the very skill you are now developing—contributes more to reading comprehension than any other factor, more even than intelligence. Every frame in this text and a majority of the review exercises are designed to cultivate top-level skill in using context.

Part II: Word Parts. Here you have four subtests, each revealing an important aspect of your use of word parts. Notice your four scores.

IIA: Memorization. This test measures your present rote knowledge of the common meanings of selected prefixes and roots. For most learners, this is the usual beginning step in the mastery of word elements. Your score on this part will suggest how many you already know. Again, the lower your score, the more room for improvement—and the better you can plan your learning efforts.

IIB: Identification. It is not enough, however, to memorize the fact, say, that *ad-* means "to or toward." You must know how to identify the presence of prefixes, roots, and suffixes as they appear in words. This is much more difficult. Not every word beginning with the letters *ad* contains the prefix *ad-*. Take the word *adynamic*. The first two letters are indeed *ad-*. But that word contains the prefix *a*, meaning "not." Add *a-* to *dynamic* and you get *adynamic*, meaning "not" dynamic. The *ad-* beginning has nothing to do with the prefix *ad-*. Furthermore, the words *abbreviate, attract, associate, annex, ascent, afferent, accumulate, arrive, allude, agglutinate,* and *append*—none of which begin with *ad-,*—all contain a form of that most changeable of prefixes, the prefix *ad-*.

Obviously, identifying word parts accurately in words is not an easy step, although a necessary one. As you work through this text, however, that step will gradually become much easier. Soon you should have little or no trouble spotting both *pre-* and *ad-* in such a word as *prearrange.*

If you're better than average in identifying word parts but below average in rote learning, you know where to put the emphasis for best progress. If you know the elements but can't identify them accurately in words, that means an entirely different emphasis.

IIC: Application. This is a measure of that all-important payoff step. If you know the meanings of word parts and can identify them in words, can you use that knowledge to define unknown words containing a familiar word part? This particular test contains words that occur no more than once in a million words. But all these relatively rare words do contain one of the prefixes or roots from section IIA. How many of these strange words did you define accurately by leaning heavily on knowledge of word parts? Here you should not be satisfied with less than 100 percent. The in-depth, chapter-by-chapter, study of elements which follows should gradually bring the insights and techniques needed for superior skill in application.

Notice how you should deal with test items in this category (cf. page 13). Take the following item:

Accolade means (1) change; (2) remedy; (3) mystery; (4) refrain; (5) award.

Suppose you know that *accolade* contains a form of the prefix *ad-*, and know further that *ad-* means "to" or "toward." How well can you apply that knowledge with that test item? In other words, which of the five choices is closest in meaning to the "to, toward" concept? Well, *change* can be either "to" or "away." With *remedy*, "for" seems closer than "to." The most natural connection with *mystery* is "about." With *refrain*, "from" seems a natural combination. But an *award* is given "to" someone, as a move "toward" recognizing some service or accomplishment. That fits best so far.

In short, when you apply your knowledge properly, you should arrive at *award* as the meaning of *accolade*. And after making that thoughtful effort you should also remember the meaning of *accolade* more easily. No wonder it's called a payoff step.

IID: Generalization. With far too much of our learning we stop with the application or payoff step. When we do, we overlook the step that brings a superpayoff. If you can generalize well, you can, in a sense, learn thousands of additional word parts never once mentioned in these pages. Only when you begin to generalize can you begin to capitalize to the full on basic rules and principles and make quantum leaps in vocabulary growth. This last test attempts to measure how well you now generalize about the behavior of imaginary prefixes or relatively rare roots. How well did you score? That score will suggest how much attention to give to this last important step.

II: Total. Add the four word-part subtest scores together to get a total score which will suggest your overall ability to deal with word parts.

III: Dictionary. The third and last diagnostic test measures how accurately you use the dictionary. The lower your score here, the more attention you should give to the prefatory section in your dictionary. Sometimes it is called, "Explanatory Notes," sometimes, "Guide to the Dictionary." But whatever it is called, study it carefully. You want information, not misinformation, when you consult your dictionary, which should be a good college-level dictionary.

So much for your three-part diagnostic check. Use the results to direct your efforts to the things needing most attention. The insights from such a diagnosis are prime factors in insuring best results. When you know your problem—your strengths and weaknesses—you can take the right steps to eliminate the difficulties. If you don't, you have to work blindly—hardly the way to make progress.

THE FOURTEEN WORDS

Now for the Fourteen Words That Make All the Difference, the fourteen words to be studied in depth in the remainder of this book. Remember: they contain the most useful shortcuts yet discovered to a bigger vocabulary.

Don't stop to memorize these elements. You don't need to. Let the rest of the book do that work for you. You'll find an entire chapter covering each prefix and root listed below.

THE FOURTEEN WORDS

Keys to the meanings of over 14,000 words

		Derivations		
Words	*Prefix*	*Common Meaning*	*Root*	*Common Meaning*
1. precept	*pre-*	(before)	*capere*	(take, seize)
2. detain	*de-*	(away, down)	*tenere*	(hold, have)
3. intermittent	*inter-*	(between, among)	*mittere*	(send)
4. offer	*ob-*	(against, to, toward)	*ferre*	(bear, carry)
5. insist	*in-*	(into)	*stare*	(stand)
6. monograph	*mono-*	(alone, one)	*graphein*	(write)
7. epilogue	*epi-*	(upon)	*legein*	(say, study of)
8. aspect	*ad-*	(to, towards)	*specere*	(see)
9. uncomplicated	*un-*	(not)	*plicare*	(fold)
	com-	(together, with)		
10. nonextended	*non-*	(not)	*tendere*	(stretch)
	ex-	(out, beyond)		
11. reproduction	*re-*	(back, again)	*ducere*	(lead)
	pro-	(forward, for)		
12. indisposed	*in-*	(not)	*ponere*	(put, place)
	dis-	(apart, not)		
13. oversufficient	*over-*	(above)	*facere*	(make, do)
	sub-	(under)		
14. mistranscribe	*mis-*	(wrong)	*scribere*	(write)
	trans-	(across, beyond)		

For best results, think through each frame in the following chapters of this book. Take the following frame from the chapter on *mono-* as an example.

A one-legged creature is a _____pode.

It is easy to fill in the right answer (*mono-*) and hurry on to the next frame. If you do, however, you are not taking full advantage of observations that may well double the effectiveness of the text. A more thoughtful look at that frame should give you reason to suspect that *pode* means "leg" – "one-legged" equals *monopode*.

Put a check in the margin by such frames. When you finish the entire unit, check your assumptions with the dictionary, in this case by looking up *pode*. This will acquaint you with the Greek word *pous, podos,* meaning "foot." This in turn brings such words as *tripod, podium, pleopod, podagra, podiatrist,* and *podophyllin* into sharper focus. This is why you should reason your way carefully through even the most obvious frames to make certain you note all pertinent relationships.

Opportunities for review are also frequently introduced. Take full advantage of them. Note the following frame from the unit on *pro-*:

> If **regress** means "to go back," and **egress,** "to go out,"
> "to go forward" would be to make ＿＿＿*gress.*

This single frame provides four opportunities: (1) to review the meaning of *re-*, (2) to preview the meaning of *e-*, (3) to reason out the meaning of *pro-*, and (4) to arrive at a meaning for *gress.*

As soon as you have written down your answer, check its correctness *immediately.* Research points up the importance of that immediate check.

Whenever you miss an item, go back over the preceding few frames to see what clues you apparently missed. Your ability to concentrate and think should show improvement along with increased word power—all three so essential to effective living in this print-filled world.

PART TWO

PREFIXES

1

OVER–
(plus Managing the Mechanics
and Mnemonics)

Here's your first prefix shortcut, *over-*, with two fringe benefits added to make the chapter even more useful. The resulting three-in-one combination helps you (1) get the most from the programmed format, (2) speed your learning through mnemonics or associations, and (3) see more fully the vocabulary-building potential of *over-*.

Take the programmed format. Only by managing it properly can you make this text more effective than an ordinary text. That means reading with a three-by-five-inch card to cover the answers in the margin.

Uncover each answer *after* you've read the frame and written your response. That makes the real difference — checking *after* making your response. Now try the first frame. Be sure the answer in the margin is covered.

1. If the word *mnemonics* comes from a Greek word meaning "to remember," you would expect

memory

mnemonics to be defined as "the art or science of improving one's ___ory."

Did you write your response before moving the card down to uncover the answer? That's how you insure best results.

Whenever you miss an item, reread the frame to see what contextual clues you overlooked. For example, knowing that *mnemonics* came from a Greek word meaning "to remember" should lead you to *memory* as the correct answer.

known

2. One important way to aid memory is by associating what you want to learn—the unknown—with what you've already learned—the _____.

It's been said that you can learn any subject with a logical structure in half the time and with half the effort by using a programmed approach. That's why you should do each frame carefully before checking the answer. You don't want to lose any of the learning advantages.

associations

3. In learning any and all prefixes and roots, therefore, use the principles of mnemonics to establish meaningful asso_____ between the known and the unknown.

Those first two frames introduced you to the concept of mnemonics and gave you a definition of that word. The third frame moved you beyond a narrow response to a general rule, useful not only with the thirty-four elements to be studied in depth but in hundreds of other learning situations.

The next step lies in moving from theory to practice, from knowing to applying. Knowing what a gun is doesn't make you an expert marksman. Similarly, knowing what mnemonics means doesn't make you able to apply that principle effectively.

The next frames are intended to speed your progress from knowing to applying, with the focus on *over-*, perhaps the easiest prefix of all to deal with.

4. If you're driving under an overpass, the overpass is not below you but _____ you.

above

5. That can be "above" in the sense of location, as with *overpass* or *overhead,* or "above" in the sense of rank or power, as in which of the following words: *overhang, overseer,* or *overcritical?*

overseer

6. But *over-* has still another meaning—that of going "beyond" or "across," as in which of the following words: *overlord, overbearing,* or *overrun?*

overrun

7. *Over-* is also used to describe movement to a lower or inferior position, as in which of the following words: *overflow, overheat, overlap,* or *overstep.*

overflow

8. But perhaps the most common meaning of all for *over-* is the meaning "excessive" or "too much," as in which of the following words: *overeat, overlook, overdue,* or *overalls.*

overeat

9. To make you better able to remember those four meanings, use *able* as a mnemonic or association device: **a** = above
   b = _____
   l = lower
   e = excessive

beyond

10. One unabridged dictionary contains over 2,000 words with *over-*. What a useful shortcut! Further-

more, *over-* is one of those rare prefixes which you can add to hundreds of words besides those actually found in the dictionary. For example, if a certain group is excessively militant, call it an ____ militant group, even if that word is not found in the dictionary.

*over*militant

11. When you know that *over-* has not one but ____ common meanings, you can deal much more easily and accurately with all words containing *over-*.

four

12. And you don't have to be overstudious, overindustrious, or overworked to remember those four meanings if you use the word ____ as your mnemonic device, your acronym.

able

Now mnemonics, or the use of associations to help you remember, is such an important aid that it deserves special added attention. So before going on with the elements to be studied in depth in the following chapters, practice using mnemonics with some other elements of almost equal value as vocabulary-building shortcuts. That special practice will help you apply mnemonics more effectively with all the key elements to follow.

13. To remember that *homo-* means "same," associate it with _____ milk — milk that is the same throughout, not separating into cream.

homogenized

14. To remember that *hydro-* means "water," think of a fire engine next to a red fire _____ to which the hose is connected.

hydrant

15. To remember that *hypo-* means "under," just think of where the doctor puts the *hypo*_____ needle when he gives you a shot in the arm.

hypo*dermic*

16. To remember that *hyper-* means "over" or "be-
    yond," think of someone who is sensitive far be-
    yond the supersensitive — someone who is _____-
    sensitive.

    *hyper*sensitive

17. To remember that *syn-* means "with or together,"
    think of *synthesis*, the putting _____ of parts or
    elements to make a whole.

    together

18. To remember that *dia-* means "through" or
    "across," just visualize a circle and the line passing
    directly through the center, the line we call the
    _____.

    diameter

19. To remember that *para-* means "beside," visualize
    two _____ lines, lines that run side by side
    without meeting.

    parallel

20. To remember that *per-* means "through," think of
    brewing coffee in a _____ in which boiling
    water bubbles up through a tube.

    percolater

21. To remember that *ab-* means "away," think of be-
    ing away from class, or being ab____.

    ab*sent*

In the preceding frame you were given the prefix and a
word to serve as a possible mnemonic. With these or
other word parts, however, remember that selecting
your own mnemonic is usually better than using one
selected by someone else.

In the next frames, prefix meanings are *not* given. You
have to discover the meanings for yourself by reasoning
from context. This encourages the kind of thinking
needed for the rest of the book. Then when you discover the meaning, find a suitable mnemonic to help
you remember it.

many

22. If a hexagon is a six-sided figure and a polygon is a many-sided figure, *poly-* probably means "____."

*poly*glot

23. If *glot* comes from the Greek word *glotta,* meaning "tongue," a person who speaks many languages or tongues would rightly be called a ____glot.

That's how you arrive at prefix or root meanings without your dictionary. Just lean on context. And if that doesn't work, try this suggestion. Think of other words containing the strange element; then look for a common idea in the words. For example, what does *mega-* mean? Think of a megaphone or a megaton bomb, then look for an idea common to them both. By thought alone you should come close to the correct definition: "large," "great," "powerful." Now try the next ones.

around

24. If in a submarine a periscope lets you look around, you would infer that *peri-* probably means "a-_____."

far

25. If a microscope is an instrument for looking at small objects, and a telescope for looking at far objects, *tele-* probably means "____."

first
original

26. If an archetype is the first or original type, *archi-* probably means "_____" or "_____."

*ante*cedents

27. When you want to remember that *ante-* means "before," think of your ancestors or ____cedents— those who came before you.

antiaircraft

28. *Anti-,* on the other hand, means "against," as in the type of gun used against aircraft, called _____.

29. The meaning of *en-* is easily remembered if you think that enclose and the less common inclose both mean "to close __."

in

30. If a tricycle has three wheels, you can easily infer, from *bicycle,* that the prefix *bi-* means "___."

two

31. To remember that *mal-* means "bad" or "badly," think of the word which means "badly adjusted," as in the sentence, "The student was socially ——————."

maladjusted

So much for Unit I. You should now feel much better acquainted with the prefix *over-* and know exactly how to manage the programmed format and how to use mnemonics, together with reason and context, to speed further progress.

Prefix Mini-Review

Except for *over-,* the first of the twenty prefixes to be studied in depth, all the prefixes mentioned in this chapter were given only brief attention. For that reason you should review them from time to time, using the following review procedures. Actually you have three review possibilities, each a bit more difficult than the preceding.

1. For your initial review, cover the right-hand column with your three-by-five-inch card. See if you can supply the common meaning. When you have, check immediately by moving your card to reveal the answer.
2. If you can do that perfectly, try a somewhat more difficult review. Cover *both* right-hand columns. See if you can supply both the suggested mnemonic and the common meaning.
3. And for the third and most difficult review, cover the two left-hand columns. See if you can supply the prefix and mnemonic association for each specified common meaning. Again, check your answers immediately.

As you can see, these mini-reviews are actually speed reviews and should quickly bring mastery. Review as often as needed to keep a perfect score.

Prefix	Suggested Mnemonic	Common Meaning
1. *homo-*	homogenized	same
2. *hydro-*	hydrant	water
3. *hypo-*	hypodermic	under
4. *hyper-*	hypersensitive	over or beyond
5. *dia-*	diameter	through
6. *para-*	parallel	beside
7. *per-*	percolator	through
8. *ab-*	absent	away
9. *poly-*	polygon	many
10. *peri-*	periscope	around
11. *tele-*	telescope	far
12. *archi-*	archetype	first or original
13. *ante-*	antecedent	before
14. *anti-*	antiaircraft	against
15. *en-*	enclose	in
16. *bi-*	bicycle	two
17. *mal-*	maladjusted	bad or badly
18. *tri-*	tricycle	three
19. *syn-*	synthesis	with or together
20. *over-*	overpass, overseer, overflow, overeat	above, beyond, lower, excessive

Opposites Review Test

For still another kind of review, try this opposites exercise. It provides an ideal way to get better acquainted with these prefix meanings. Pairing any word or word part with its opposite brings added understanding, largely because of the extra thought demanded. Harness that extra thought power to heighten your proficiency and familiarity with the prefixes just covered.

In addition, some important vocabulary tests that you may take ask for opposites instead of synonyms. This type of exercise will prepare you to handle such tests more effectively.

For the following ten-item review, pick the choice that most nearly means the opposite. (Answers are on page 255.)

Look at the following example:

The opposite of *poly-* is (1) square; (2) round; (3) many; (4) few.

If you know that *poly-* means "many," you'll have no trouble picking the opposite — "few" — as the right answer. Do the following in the same way.

1. The opposite of *tele-* is   (1) sight; (2) near; (3) far; (4) sound.

2. The opposite of *en-* is   (1) in; (2) for; (3) around; (4) out.

3. The opposite of *archi-* is   (1) last; (2) first; (3) straight; (4) curved.

4. The opposite of *mal-* is   (1) major; (2) minor; (3) good; (4) bad.

5. The opposite of *hyper-* is   (1) over; (2) under; (3) wide; (4) narrow.

Did you notice the extra thought power needed?

For the next five, think first of the word-part meaning, then of the opposite. Lastly, look for the definition closest to that opposite meaning.

6. The opposite of *synonym* is   (1) acronym; (2) name; (3) similarity; (4) antonym.

7. The opposite of *megacephaly* is   (1) loss of hearing; (2) smallness of head; (3) big feet; (4) arm paralysis.

8. The opposite of *perimeter* is   (1) line around an area; (2) line through an area; (3) circular figure; (4) rectangular figure.

9. The opposite of *hydrofoil* is   (1) dune buggy; (2) boat; (3) container; (4) aluminum wrapping.

10. The opposite of *antinomy* is   (1) an allowance; (2) agreement of two laws; (3) contrary viewpoint; (4) metallic compound.

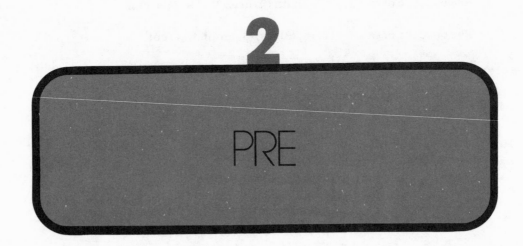

Pre- is the second prefix to be studied in depth. Some additional guidance will still be provided, however, to insure maximum results from your efforts.

The first frame suggests how you can determine the meaning of any prefix, using *pre-* as an example.

before

1. If *preview* means "to view before" and *preheat,* "to heat before," you would assume *pre-* means "_____."

prefix

2. But *before* has several shades of meaning. In which one of the following words, for example, does *pre-* have the meaning "before in place," "front," "anterior"?
prescribe
prewar
prefix

3. In which one of the following words does *pre-* mean "before in time," "previously"?
   prefer
   prearrange
   pretend

   prearrange

4. In which one of the following words does *pre-* mean "before others in rank or degree"?
   preeminent
   precancel
   preliminary

   preeminent

Knowing prefix meaning or shades of meaning, however, is only a start. The next problem is identifying the prefix in its normal setting—a word. The next four frames will help you discover an important rule of thumb—a principle you can put to immediate use with all prefixes.

5. Which of the following words are *still* words when you take off the *pre-*?
   precast   preschool
   pretzel   press

   precast
   preschool

6. Which two words would you infer do *not* contain the prefix *pre-*?
   precast   preschool
   pretzel   press

   pretzel
   press

Apparently the prefix *pre-* is found in most but not all words beginning with the letters *p, r, e*.

7. If *preschool* and *precast* both contain the prefix *pre-*, apparently one way to check the presence of a prefix is to determine if what follows the supposed prefix is a _____.

   word

Apply this newly learned rule to speed your move from theory right into practice.

prenominate

8. With that rule of thumb in mind, which of the following words probably contains the prefix *pre-*?

preternatural   prenominate
prester   preach

Of course, two checks are better than one, especially if neither covers all situations. The following frames give you a second rule of thumb.

preclude

9. In which of the following words can you substitute another prefix, such as *in-*, for the prefix *pre-*?

preclude
predator

preclude

10. Which of the following words probably contains the prefix *pre-*?

preclude
pretty
pressure

prefix

11. Now you have an additional rule-of-thumb check on the presence of a prefix. See if another _____ can be substituted in its place.

prefix

12. Taking off the *pre-* in *preclude* does not leave a word, *but* substituting another _____ for *pre-* will make a different word.

Always try both rule-of-thumb checks. If either or both work, you have reason to suspect the presence of a prefix.

It is not enough to know prefix meanings and be able to identify their presence in words. You must still take the payoff step—the useful application of this knowledge in dealing both with familiar and strange words.

This knowledge should also let you make generalizations which apply with equal force to *thousands* of prefixes not specifically dealt with here.

In the following frames put your prefix knowledge to work in a variety of common situations.

13. Prefix knowledge makes familiar words more interesting. Take *prelude*. The prefix reminds us that a prelude is something played _____ the main performance begins.

    before

14. If *post-* means "after," as in *postscript* or *postpone*, something played after the main performance would be appropriately called, not a prelude, but a _____.

    postlude

15. And strange words become less so with prefix knowledge to apply. If you hear that someone has a predilection for jazz, the prefix suggests he puts it _____ other kinds of music.

    before

16. In bridge, a preemptive bid is designed to get you the bid _____ your opponents have a chance to communicate information about their hands.

    before

17. Your knowledge of *pre-* can help you define a *prelate* as a
    layman
    high-ranking clergyman
    church member.

    high-ranking
    clergyman
    (before others
    in rank)

18. And a prefect is probably
    a newspaper reporter
    an administrative official
    a policeman.

    an administrative
    official

Selecting the appropriate word to fit a given context is still another facet of word power. Most of the remaining frames encourage you to come up with the *pre-* word that fits the context.

preamble

19. We speak of the "before" part of a constitution as the _____ of the constitution.

president

20. In this country, the man "before" all others in our national government is called the _____.

preface

21. The "before" part of a book—usually found even before the introduction—is called the _____.

forewarn him

22. If you premonish someone, you would infer you
   advise him
   help him
   forewarn him.

first name

23. *Pre-* comes from the Latin *prae*, meaning "before." In ancient Rome, a man had three names. His prae-nomen would be his

   first name
   second name
   last name.

prepare

24. To make ready beforehand for a situation is to _____ for it.

prejudiced

25. If someone judges a matter before he has sufficient evidence or knowledge, he is spoken of as a _____ individual.

This unit, like most of those that follow, is intended to teach four things: (1) what the prefix commonly means, with attention to important shades of meaning; (2) how to identify its presence in a word through use of two practical rule-of-thumb principles; (3) how to apply knowledge of its meaning to make familiar words more interesting and strange words more understandable and memorable; (4) how to select appropriate words for a given context and develop added fluency with such words.

Now you've finished your in-depth study of one prefix. How useful is *pre-* as a shortcut to word meanings? To find out, turn to a good collegiate dictionary. In one desk-sized dictionary, for example, you'll find *over seven pages* of words between the entry for *pre-* and *prexy*, the last word with *pre-*. You'll find many more, of course, in the big unabridged dictionary—*over fifteen larger-sized pages,* to be exact, between *pre-* and *prezone.*

In addition, each specialized field has words found only in specialized dictionaries. *Stedman's Medical Dictionary,* for example, contains 139 words with *pre-*, no one of which is found in a collegiate dictionary.

Such *pre*ponderous evidence demonstrates its *pre*eminent importance! Don't *pre*sume to let any *pre*text *pre*vent you from capitalizing on its *pre*sence. Attention to word parts provides an ideal *pre*scription for successful vocabulary development. *Pre-* is indeed an invaluable aid.

You need not rely on premonitions or presentiments to build your vocabulary. Just start applying your prefix knowledge to cope with strange or new words, such as the following.

1. If you decide to *prelect,* you'll need to   (1) join a church; (2) get before an audience; (3) become a policeman; (4) be nominated.   1. _____

2. A *precursor* is a   (1) blasphemer; (2) minister; (3) helper; (4) forerunner.   2. _____

3. *Precocious* means   (1) slow-starting;   (2) before average; (3) new; (4) worn.   3. _____

4. A *prefect* is a   (1) sworn statement; (2) student; (3) chief official; (4) soldier.

4. _____

5. *Predilection* means   (1) abbreviation; (2) gift; (3) token; (4) preference.

5. _____

Keep the prefix meaning in mind. To *prelect* is to lecture "before" a group. A *precursor* is one or that which goes "before" something. A *precocious* child is one who has matured "before" the average. A *prefect* is an official "before" others in rank. And if you have a *predilection* for something, you favor it "before" other things. For more information, look up the words in your dictionary.

To speed your learning of key prefixes, roots, and suffixes, *spaced* review apparently works best, especially if you have a variety of review types. That's why you'll find review exercises—verbal analogies, opposites, sentence completions, context, and the like—interspersed between units instead of being grouped all together.

3

DE

1. Some prefixes, such as *pre-*, have only one common meaning. Others, such as *de-*, have several. You would infer from the words *descend* and *depress* that one meaning of *de-* is ____, the opposite of "up."

   down

2. That is why, when you look "down" on someone with disfavor or contempt, you may be said to __spise him.

   *de*spise

3. You should be able to arrive at another common meaning of *de-* through the word *depart*. Depart does not mean "to go down" as much as it does "to go a___."

   a*way*

4. Here is another example with this meaning of *de-*. When you take "away" the trailer that is attached to your car, you are said to _____ it.

   detach

47

5. Still a third common meaning of *de-* is that of "reversing," "undoing," or "freeing from." In which of the following words is that meaning dominant?

defrost

detail

defrost

detect

6. Here is still another example of that meaning. Usually before a coded message can be understood, someone must de＿＿＿＿ it.

*de*code

7. Or take gas which is compressed into a small cylinder. When you release or free it, you ＿＿compress it.

*de*compress

8. Finally, *de-* is sometimes used as an intensive, to catch the idea of "entirely" or "completely," as in *denude* — to make entirely or ＿＿＿＿＿＿＿＿＿ nude.

completely

9. If a soldier deserts his post, which meaning of *de-* is uppermost?

down or away

entirely

reverse

down or away

10. If you are strongly inclined to turn "down" an invitation, you will probably de＿＿＿＿＿ to go.

*de*cline

11. Some foreigners found guilty of a crime are not imprisoned but taken to the nearest port and de＿＿＿＿＿＿ to their native land.

*de*ported

12. To get the reverse of *accelerate* (or speed up) just change the prefix. To slow down is to ＿＿＿＿＿＿＿＿＿.

decelerate

13. Put your prefix knowledge to use with *detruncate*.
You would expect it to mean   to cut down

to cut down   to fill in
to draw up   to grow big.

14. In a military operation, when you deploy your men
you probably   spread them out
feed them   (or away)
draft them
spread them out.

15. With all the meanings in mind—down or away,
reverse, entirely—you would assume *devolve* would
mean   to pass

to consider
to pass
to remain.

16. When a train jumps "away" from the rails, we say it
is _____.   derailed

17. When you are forced to leave the highway because
of road repairs, you turn "away" on a _____.   detour

18. Remembering that prefixes are often added to existing words to make new words, which one of the
following words probably contains the prefix *de*-?   deform
deuce
deform
dental

19. Remembering that other prefixes can usually be
substituted in words containing a prefix, which one
of the following words probably does *not* contain
the prefix *de*-?   demon
demon
deform
defer

delegate

20. Someone sent "away" to a convention as a representative is spoken of as a de_____.

away

21. If you delete a word from a letter, you take it a___.

deflate

22. The reverse of *inflate* is _____.

deficiency

23. A shortage or deficit is also spoken of as a _____-iency.

decrease

24. The reverse of *increase* is _____.

deducted

25. In conducting business affairs, remember that on income tax returns certain amounts can be taken "away" or de_____.

deteriorating

26. Word from abroad suggested that things were rapidly going "down" from bad to worse. In short, they were _____ing.

Mini-Review

Remember to cover the last two columns. See if you can supply all four meanings of *de-*.

Prefix	Suggested Mnemonic	Common Meaning
1. *de-*	depress	down
2. *de-*	depart	away
3. *de-*	defrost	reverse or undo
4. *de-*	denude	entirely or completely

As a further review, try to unlock the meanings of *defenestration*, *desuetude*, *defalcate*, *demise*, and *defray*. Since they appear only about once in a million words, if you know even one, your vocabulary would be exceptional.

Lean on prefix knowledge for help with this difficult test. Pick the nearest synonym. (Answers are on page 255.)

1. _____

1. "You say he died from *defenestration?* Too bad! He shouldn't have   (1) eaten so much; (2) lifted such a heavy load; (3) driven so fast; (4) thrown himself down from the tenth-story window."

2. _____

2. *Desuetude* means   (1) smoothness; (2) disuse; (3) maturity; (4) sun.

3. _____

3. *Defalcate* means   (1) deafen; (2) earn; (3) embezzle; (4) acquire.

4. _____

4. *Demise* means   (1) opening; (2) death; (3) demon; (4) rule.

5. _____

5. *Defray* means   (1) pay; (2) collect; (3) budget; (4) itemize.

Verbal Analogy Review Test

Have you ever taken an analogy test? Such a test demands more than a knowledge of word meaning. It tests your ability to see relationships and to reason accurately as well as to show off your word power. Analogy tests are considered by some as a way of measuring intelligence, since they demand accurate insights into relationships between ideas, as represented by words.

Try the following items for additional review of *pre-* and *de-* and to improve your skill and acquaintance with this kind of test. Often on an application blank you have a line indicated for your surname. If you don't know what *surname* means you may make a mistake that could cost you the job. Look at this sample item to see how the analogy-type item works.

Praenomen is to *first name* as *surname* is to ____ *name.*

The pattern established by the first part is: *word* is to *word meaning.* You must follow an analogous pattern with the next part. That means you must supply the word meaning for *surname,* which is the *last* or family name. Do the next items in the same way. (Answers are on page 255.)

1. *Preview* is to *view before* as *preheat* is to ____ _____.

2. *Preface* is to *beginning* as *appendix* is to _____.

3. *Presage* is to *foretell* as *precursor* is to ____ *runner.*

4. *Prefix* is to *suffix* as *prelude* is to *post* ____.

5. *Pre-* is to *before* as *de-* is to *d*___ or *a*___.

6. *Decrease* is to *increase* as *deflate* is to _____.

7. *Decode* is to *code* as *defrost* is to _____.

8. *Detach* is to *attach* as *decelerate* is to _____.

9. *Detruncate* is to *de-* as *preemptive* is to ___.

10. *Desiccate* is to *remove moisture* as *denude* is to _____ *covering.*

4

MONO

1. The Greek word *monos* means "one," "single," or "alone." If *lithos* means "stone," then a single stone shaped into a statue or monument would appropriately be called a _____lith.

    *mono*lith

2. If a democracy is government by the people, government by one person is rightly named a _____cracy.

    *mono*cracy

3. If marriage to many is *polygamy*, marriage to one would be _____.

    *mono*gamy

4. How many colors would you expect to see in a monochrome? ___

    one

5. How many limbs are paralyzed in a monoplegia case?

    one

monaxial

6. The prefix *mono-* has two forms. It usually drops the final *o* before roots beginning with a vowel. For example, if *mono-* is added to *axial,* a root beginning with a vowel, the resulting combination should be spelled _____.

monarch

7. The single or sole ruler of a state—sometimes called king or emperor—may also be called a ___arch.

one

8. In biology, the term *monad* is used to describe any organism that consists of only ___ cell.

monastery

9. When someone becomes a monk and retires from the world because of religious vows, his place of residence is called a ___astery.

monanthous

10. If the Greek word *anthos* means "flower," the botanical term for a plant having only one flower would be ___anthous.

monocarp

11. Keeping the two forms, *mono-* and *mon-,* in mind and remembering the final *o* is dropped before a root beginning with a vowel, determine which one of the following words probably contains the prefix *mono-.*

montage   mongrel
monstrous   monocarp

monocle

12. The Latin word *oculus* means "eye." An eyeglass for one eye, formerly worn by Englishmen, is appropriately called a _____.

monosyllabic

13. Words of one syllable are called ____syllabic words.

14. As opposed to the polygenesis theory of the origin of life, there is the belief that all life descended from a "single" original organism. It is called the _____ theory.

monogenesis

15. In business, the exclusive control of a commodity or service is called a _____.

monopoly

16. If a *phobia* is an abnormal fear, an abnormal fear of being alone is appropriately called a _____.

monophobia

17. The Greek noun *pous, podos,* means "foot." In the word *monopode, mono-* is the prefix, and *pode,* the base, or r__t, to which prefix and suffix elements are added.

root

18. In the word *podophyllin, pod* is in the position of and used as a _____, not a root.

prefix

19. A one-legged creature is a ____pode.

*mono*pode

20. The dictionary classifies word parts as prefix, root, suffix, or combining form. With *pous, podos,* used in both a prefix and root position, you would expect it to be classified, not as a prefix or root, but as a _____ ____.

combining form

21. The Greek word *mania* means "madness." A craze or mania for some one thing is a _____.

monomania

22. How many actors would you expect to see in a monodrama? ___

one

23. If life seems to continue along in "one" way, with scarcely any variation, we call it mono_____.

mono*tonous*

monogram

24. If *gram* is a combining form meaning "something written," as in *telegram,* you would call a "single" figure or design made up of two or more letters a
    _____.

*mononucle*osis

25. The presence in the blood of an abnormal number of leucocytes having only *one* nucleus is a condition called _____osis.

Remember that if an element such as *gram* is found in *gram*ophone as well as tele*gram*, it is neither a prefix nor root but a combining form.

5

INTER

1. *Inter-* comes from the Latin word *inter,* meaning "between" or "among." Action "between" two things would therefore properly be called an _____-action.

   *inter*action

2. When you add *pre-* to *empt* to make *preempt,* you keep both *e*'s. In the same way, when you add *inter-* to *racial,* you should spell the resulting combination _____.

   interracial

3. If a *prelude* is something "played before" a performance, and *postlude,* something "played after" a performance, something "played between" acts should be called an _____.

   interlude

4. With *inter-,* one problem is to distinguish between *inter-,* and the prefix *in-* added to a word beginning

interpose
(expose)

with *ter*. In which of the following can you make a new word by substituting another prefix, such as *ex-*, for the five-letter prefix *inter-*?

interpose
internal

5. In which of the words can you substitute another prefix for *in-*?
interpose
internal
––––––––.

internal
(external)

6. If prefix substitution doesn't work, try a suffix. Take the word *interminable*. Is the prefix *in-* or *inter-*? Try substituting a suffix, such as *-ate*, in place of *-able*. Which resulting combination is a word—*terminate* or *minate*? ––––––––

terminate

7. This rule-of-thumb check is a reminder that both prefixes and ––––––––– are added to roots to make words.

suffixes

8. The Latin word *terminus* means "limit," "boundary," or "end." Drop the *-us* ending to get the common root form, *termin*. When you bring something to an "end" or conclusion, you termin–––– it.

term*inate*

9. One who acts is an actor. In like manner, one who or that which terminates something is a ––––––––––.

terminator

10. The "end" of a railroad line or airline is spoken of as a terminus or termin––.

termin*al*

11. Sometimes a root such as *termin* is shortened even farther. Part of *termin* names the stipulated length for holding an office, that is, the –––––– of office.

term

12. A few suffixes may even be added to this shortened form. For example, a limitless or boundless term of office could be called term____.

    term*less*

13. Word-analysis insights will develop rapidly as you manipulate these prefix, root, and _____ elements in this way.

    suffix

14. And word parts help you define and remember words more easily. *Interim,* for example, probably means that period of time
    before
    between
    after.

    between

15. The period of time "between" two events is called the time _____val.

    *inter*val

16. If *erupt* means literally "to break out," and *disrupt,* "to break apart," what word means "to break between," as in conversation? _____

    interrupt

17. If things are scattered here and there "among" other things, they are _____spersed.

    *inter*spersed

18. The region "between" planets is the _____-__ary region.

    *interplanet*ary

19. The time "between" acts or parts of a play or concert is called the _____.

    intermission

20. In anatomy or zoology, the part "between" two nodes is called the _____.

    internode

21. One who tries to hinder or prevent the delivery of the message wants to _____cept it.

    *inter*cept

*inter*cede

22. When you go to the leader of a labor union to plead for one of the members, you can be said to _____-cede for him.

international

23. An agreement between or among nations is spoken of as an _____ agreement.

insert new words

24. When you interpolate something in a manuscript you probably

insert new words   condense
rephrase   study it.

converses

25. An interlocutor would be one who

converses   drives
studies   stands.

intermediator

26. Someone acting as mediator between two parties would be an _____ or intermediary.

b*etween* or a*mong*

27. One last reminder—*inter*- commonly means "b_____" or "a____."

Review Test I

A. In the blank after the prefix in the left-hand column, write the number, from the right-hand list, of the common meaning of the prefix. The same meaning may apply to more than one prefix. Some meanings will not be used at all.

1. *pre-*   _____

2. *de-*   _____

3. *mono-*   _____

4. *inter-*   _____

5. *ab-* or *abs-* _____ .

1. beside
2. between, among
3. out, outside
4. through
5. away, down
6. away
7. before
8. alone, one

B. In each of the following sets of words, there is one word that does *not* contain the prefix found in the rest of the words in that set. Using the principles from Unit 2, find that word and enter the appropriate number in the blank at the right.

1. (1) pretzel; (2) pretext; (3) prefer; (4) prebake   1. _____

2. (1) deserve; (2) detain; (3) desist; (4) derrick   2. _____

3. (1) monorail; (2) monaxial; (3) mongrel; (4) monologue   3. _____

4. (1) intercede; (2) intern; (3) interweave; (4) interlude   4. _____

5. (1) abeam; (2) abnormal; (3) abrupt; (4) abject   5. _____

C. Use your knowledge of prefixes to help you define the relatively strange words in the following vocabulary test. Enter the appropriate number in the blank at the right to identify the synonym.

1. *Prevision* means (1) instruction; (2) foresight; (3) special showing; (4) beauty.   1. _____

2. *Deterge* means to (1) fill; (2) start; (3) raise; (4) cleanse.   2. _____

3. *Monopode* means (1) derailed; (2) one-footed; (3) magnified; (4) crossbones.   3. _____

4. *Interpolate* means (1) lengthen; (2) check up; (3) arouse; (4) insert between.   4. _____

5. *Aberration* means (1) deviation from norm; (2) assistance; (3) registration; (4) correction of text.   5. _____

(*Answers on page 255.*)

Using Contextual Clues

Context—first element in the CPD formula—demands closer attention at this point. To begin, check your use of context by trying the following test, with no context to help. Put your answer in column A.

	A	B

1. *Parsimonious* means   (1) careful; (2) hasty; (3) miserly; (4) honest; (5) pious.

1. ____ ____

2. *Veracious* means   (1) varied; (2) hungry; (3) false; (4) fierce; (5) accurate.

2. ____ ____

3. *Lavaliere* means   (1) neckerchief; (2) ornament on a chain; (3) string of beads; (4) cross; (5) valve.

3. ____ ____

4. *Cryptic* means   (1) cautious; (2) clear; (3) different; (4) solid; (5) puzzling.

4. ____ ____

5. *Cynosure* means one who is   (1) critical; (2) pessimistic; (3) a focal point; (4) disappointed in life; (5) silly.

5. ____ ____

To see how well you now use context, you'll soon be given full context for each of those five words. But before that, you should know exactly what contextual clues are. Otherwise you can't put them to good use.

Contextual clues can be (1) *synonyms* or (2) *antonyms*, words or phrases meaning the same or opposite. For example, the phrase, "attention to context, or surrounding words," gives you a synonym for context—surrounding words. Sometimes context contains an actual (3) *definition*, and if not a definition, an (4) *explanation* which suggests a definition. The explanation may include helpful (5) *comparisons* or *contrasts*, with (6) *details* to contribute further understanding of a strange word. Those details may in turn establish a (7) *general mood*, or *tone*, to add more subtle understandings.

Those are the seven kinds of contextual clues you should look for in the following examples, where you can see them illustrated and labeled.

Just as Sherlock Holmes used a variety of clues to solve a mystery so should you use a variety of contextual clues to solve word-meaning mysteries. Read the following contexts, then take the same five-item test over again. Enter your new answers in column B. Perfect use of context means a perfect score. (Answers are on page 255.)

Dick, whose parents were quite *stingy*, fell into exactly the same habits himself. For that reason, later on, he found it impossible to change from a ⧄parsimonious⧄ person to an *extravagânt* one

(1) synonym

(2) antonym

Compare the two newspaper articles. You'll see that one writer presented an *untruthful account by leaving out key details*. The other article, which included all pertinent details, was a truly veracious account.

(4) explanation
5) comparison and contrast

My grandmother's lavalier was rather *heavy* for the delicate *gold chain* I had, but I wore it to the dance anyway. A friend of mine marveled that I would wear something of *such value* loosely *around my neck* while dancing.

(6) details

The cryptic words of the note left me *puzzled*. I could not fathom the *hidden or concealed meaning*.

(6) detail
(3) definition

The dancer's main object in life was *to be noticed*. That meant *dressing* in the *latest style* and *copying* the *mannerisms* of *famous movie stars*. At a party it meant trying to *dominate* the scene by *loud talk* and *grand gestures*. It was like *playing before an audience* both on and off stage. As a result, the dancer was always the cynosure of attention.

(6) details
(7) general mood or tone

That workout should help you handle context much more effectivly. This entire book, with its context-oriented programmed format will gradually make your use of such clues almost effortless and automatic.

6

UN

1. The prefix *un-* has several different meanings. If
   we are uncomfortable we are not comfortable. If a
   box is untouched it is ___ touched.

not

2. In many words we can, without changing the meaning, substitute the word *not* for the negative
   prefix __.

un-

3. If you are uncertain, you are ___ certain.

not

4. But what about *untie*? Is this a simple negative? Or
   a reversal of verb action?

a reversal of verb
action

5. In which of the following words is *un-* used to mean
   a reversal of verb action?
   unaware
   unfasten
   unclean

unfasten

6. In a few rare but interesting words, *un-* has the force of an intensive. In which of these words is the verb action intensified (not reversed)?

    unloosed
    unchained
    unrolled

    unloosed
    (same as *loosed*)

7. In which of the following words does *un-* have the force of a simple negative?

    unbraid
    unbroken
    unburden

    unbroken

8. When adding *un-* to a word or root beginning with *n*, as in *noted*, both *n*'s must be retained, giving us the correct spelling _____.

    unnoted

9. If rules are "not" unnecessary, they are, in a word,

    _____.

10. Beware of possible confusion between *un-* and the combining form *uni*, meaning "one." In which of the following does the prefix *un-* appear?

    unissued
    unipersonal

    unissued

11. In which of the following does the combining form *uni-*, meaning "one," appear?

    unison
    unimportant

    unison

12. If a vote is unanimous, all voters

    are of one mind
    did not vote
    voted one way or the other.

    are of one mind

one

13. On rare occasions, as with *unanimous*, the form may suggest the prefix *un-* but the meaning will suggest a derivation from the Latin word *unus*, meaning ___.

14. Which of the following words is apparently related to *unus* or *uni-*, meaning "one"?
    unassuming
    unequal

unique

    unique

15. Obviously most, but not all, words beginning with *un-* contain that prefix. Of the following, which word does contain that prefix?

uncivil

    uncivil
    uncle
    unction

16. If a room is not tidy or in good order, it is called

untidy

    _____.

17. If some fruit is green or immature, it can be called

unripe

    _____.

18. When you spread a flag out from a furled state, you

*un*furl

    __furl it.

19. If something cannot be thought, it is literally

*unthink*able

    _____able.

untruth

20. A falsehood is the same as an _____.

unaddressed

21. If a letter lacks an address, it is _____.

22. If one is unwary, heedless, or thoughtless, he is likely to be __aware of danger.

unaware

23. If something is not of this world, or ghostly, it can be called __earth__.

unearthly

24. Any writing not in accordance with the rules of grammar is _____.

ungrammatical

25. The middle English *kempen* means "comb." You can vary that original form to express the idea of uncombed or un_____ hair.

un*kempt*

26. To express a simple negative, a reversal or verb action or simply an intensification of action, use the prefix __.

un-

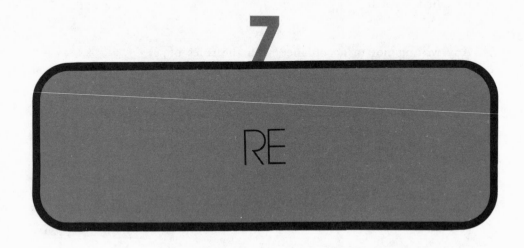

7

RE

1. The hardworking prefix *re-* has a mild case of schizophrenia, with two different meanings. When you return something, you give it b____.

back

2. When you reread something, you read it a ____.

again

3. This is not a bad case of split personality, for when you reread something, you read it again but also go b____ over it.

back

4. *Re-* is schizophrenic in still another sense, for it is both an active and passive prefix. An active _____ is one that can be added to regular words to make new words.

prefix

5. The words *group,* *heat,* and *load* are words in their own right. When you add *re-* you get *regroup, re-heat,* and _____.

reload

6. *Re-* is a passive prefix in all words where it is a necessary part and cannot be removed to leave a word. Which of the following is not a word when you remove *re-?*
   refer   reuse
   readjust   remove

refer

7. *Re-* is a passive prefix or necessary part of which of the following words?
   replace   revoke
   rerun   react

revoke

8. This distinction helps with the meaning of *re-,* for the meaning of the active *re-,* as in *reread,* is usually "_____," not "back."

again

9. The meaning of the passive *re-,* as in *revert*— when you revert to a former habit or practice—is usually "____."

back

10. If *memoir* is from a Latin word meaning "mindful" and is related to *memory,* when we bring something "back" to mind we are said to re_____ it.

re*member*

11. There are several activities that insure better memory. One is to view "again" or to _____ what you want to remember.

review

12. Figures can be cited to show that more can be remembered if one repeats aloud from memory or _____ what he has learned.

recites

*reflec*ted

13. When you look into a mirror, you see your image
    _____ed "back."

refrain

14. If *frenum* is a Latin word meaning "a rein," such
    as used to curb a horse, to hold yourself "back"
    from doing something is to _____ from doing it.

refuge

15. If *fugere* is a Latin word meaning "to flee," a shel-
    ter or safe retreat to go "back" to would be a
    _____.

refund

16. If *fundere* is a Latin word meaning "to pour," to
    repay or "pour back" would be to _____. \

letters

17. When you encounter Latin words such as *fugere*
    and *fundere,* you should habitually drop the last
    few l_____.

canceled it

18. If you rescind an order, the prefix suggests that you

    prepared it   read it
    announced it   canceled it.

stubbornly defiant

19. The *calc* in *recalcitrant* comes from *calx,* the Latin
    word meaning "heel." This, plus prefix knowledge,
    should help you define *recalcitrant* as

    cooperative   stubbornly defiant
    forward looking   completely helpless.

recapitulate

20. *To capitulate* sometimes means "to draw up into
    heads or chapters." If, at the end, you summarize or
    briefly outline what you covered, you can be said to
    _____.

receipt

21. When you pay a bill, you ordinarily receive some-
    thing "back" which acknowledges that fact. It is
    called a _____.

22. All words beginning with *re-* do not contain that
prefix. Which of the following does *not* contain a
prefix?

    reddish

   reduce   recur
   reddish   result

23. If the Latin verb *manere* means "to stay," what
word means "to stay back"? _____

    remain

24. If you are looking for words derived from the Latin
verb *mederi,* meaning "to heal," should you look
for *med* or *eri?*

    med

25. What English word is used to describe the medicine
or treatment which "heals" or restores one "back"
to health? re_____

    remedy

26. To recapitulate, the two most common meanings
of *re-* are b___ and a_____.

    b*ack* and a*gain*

As further review, take the strange words *recant, recidivist, recalcitrant, recondite,* and *replete.* Now apply
your knowledge of prefix meaning as you work through
the following short synonym test. (Answers are on
page 256.)

1. _____

   1. *Recant* means to (1) warm up; (2) take back; (3)
     speak; (4) disagree.

2. _____

   2. A *recidivist* is a (1) backslider; (2) politician; (3)
     director; (4) pioneer.

3. _____

   3. *Recalcitrant* means (1) hard; (2) powdered; (3)
     shrewd; (4) obstinate.

4. _____

   4. *Recondite* means (1) hidden; (2) wise; (3) happy;
     (4) old.

5. _____

5. *Replete* means   (1) completely filled; (2) almost finished; (3) moist; (4) dry.

To *recant* is to take "back" something you have said or believed. A tendency to go "back" to some criminal action or antisocial behavior makes one a *recidivist*. If someone is *recalcitrant,* he tends to kick "back" in an obstinate fashion. If we use words that are too abstruse, we hide the meaning—to keep it "back" out of sight. In short, we are *recondite*. After a big dinner you feel full, or *replete. Plere* means "fill" and *re-* "again" or "completely."

8

TRANS

1. *Trans-* means "across," "beyond," or "over." To transport a car from New York to San Francisco would be to take it a_____ the country.

across

2. The Latin verb *agree,* meaning "to drive," often comes over into English as *act.* If you conduct business, driving it "across" to completion, you can say you _____acted it.

*trans*acted

3. If the Latin noun *mons, montis,* means "mountain," you would expect Monte Carlo to be built on a _____.

mountain

4. A transmontane highway would probably be a road, not under, but ____ some mountains.

over

5. If the Latin verb *mutare* means "to change," the word which means "change over," as when the alchemists tried to change lead "over" into gold, is _____.

transmute

6. In a few words the final *s* of *trans-* is dropped, as in the word meaning a state resembling sleep, as in a hypnotic ____ce.

*tran*ce

7. Pills which take a person from a state of tension "over" to a quiet, calm state are called ____quilizers.

*tran*quilizers

8. Air flights "across" the Atlantic are called _____\-_____ flights.

transatlantic

9. If you know that *calere* is the Latin word meaning "heat," you would expect the word *transcalent* to mean conducting ____ readily.

heat

10. If *ascend* contains a form of *scandere*, "to climb," when you "climb beyond" the limits expected, you can be said to _____ expectations.

transcend

11. If *scribere* means "to write," when you make a written or typed copy of some shorthand notes, you are _____ing them.

*transcrib*ing

12. A copy, or reproduction, of your academic grades, because it is reproduced "over" on another sheet, is called a _____.

transcript

13. When you change the form of something, you _____ it.

transform

14. In electricity, the apparatus for changing the form of the current from high to low voltage is called a ——————.

transformer

15. When blood is transferred from one person to another, it is called a blood ——————.

transfusion

16. You would infer that the Latin word *fundere,* found in *transfusion,* probably means
to rest
to pour
to harden.

to pour

17. Someone constantly on the move and without any permanent abode would be called a —————ient.

*trans*ient

18. When someone is transformed in such a way as to exalt or glorify, he is said to be —————figured.

*trans*figured

19. If "to go forward" is *to progress* and "to go back," *to regress,* when a man goes "over" set limits so as to break a law or commit a crime, we say he has ——————.

transgressed

20. If you know that *lucere* is a Latin word meaning "to shine," you would infer that frosted glass which permits light to shine through would be called ——————.

translucent

21. The word meaning to migrate "across" from one country to another would be —————migrate.

*trans*migrate

22. If the prefix *ex-* or *e-* means "out," the word meaning "to migrate out" of a country would be ——————.

emigrate

im-
(to make
immigrate)

23. What prefix would you add to *migrate* to express the idea of moving *into* a country?

*trans*om

24. A small window or panel "across" the top of a door is called a _____om.

see through

25. Prefix knowledge should suggest that *transpicuous* means something you can
    see through
    listen to
    work at.

trans-

26. Now you should connect the meanings "across," "beyond," or "over" with the prefix _____.

1. If *regress* means "to go back," and *egress*, "to go out," "to go forward" would be to make ___gress.

   *pro*gress

2. Apparently, if *progress* means "to go forward," *pro-* means "_____."

   forward

3. Another common meaning of *pro-* is "for," in the sense of "in favor of." In which of the following words is this the meaning of *pro-*?
   produce
   prolabor
   prominent

   prolabor

4. Still a third shade of meaning is "for" in the sense of a substitute, or "in place of." A word used "for" a noun, for example, is a ___noun.

   *pro*noun

forward
for

5. From now on, whenever you see *pro-*, look for the meanings "_____" or "___."

proceed

6. If the Latin *cedere* means "to move or yield" as in *exceed*, what word means "move forward"?

_____

fore part

7. Prefix meaning should help you define *procephalic* as which part of the head?

back part   fore part
side part   top part

*pro*cession

8. When a group lines up in a long line and moves in a set fashion down the street, it is called a ___cession.

proclaim

9. If the word *claim* comes from *clamere*, meaning "to cry," *exclaim* would literally mean "cry out." What word would mean "cry forth" or "announce?"

_____

tends in that
direction

10. Your prefix knowledge should suggest that if someone has a proclivity to vice, he

shuns it   disclaims it
tends in that direction   hates it.

proconsul

11. One who serves "for" a consul and has consular authority would be called a _____.

*procras*tinate

12. If *cras* is a Latin word meaning "tomorrow," putting something "forward" to the future would be to _____tinate.

procumbent

13. If an incumbent figure is one that is lying or resting on something, what would you call a figure that is lying "forward," face down? _____

14. An extraordinary child, one who has moved "forward" faster than usual, is often spoken of as a child ___digy.

*pro*digy

15. Judging from the prefix, a *proem* is probably

 a poem   a speech
 an introduction   a summary.

an introduction

16. If the Latin word *fluere* means "to flow," as in the phrase "fluent speaker," what word probably means flowing "forward"? _____

profluent

17. *Infuse* means "pour in." One who "pours forth" apologies is _____ in apologies.

profuse

18. If *inject* means, literally, "to throw in," the word that means to throw forward is _____.

project

19. The word that names an object designed to be thrown or shot "forward" is _____ile.

*project*ile

20. If you lengthen the time, you make it longer or _____ it.

prolong

21. Something remote is literally "moved back." When you "move forward" from one position to a better one, you say you are _____.

promoted

22. If *impel* means "to drive in or into," what word means "drive forward or ahead"? _____

propel

23. Your prefix knowledge should suggest that *propensity* means

 calmness
 thought
 inclination.

inclination

in favor of

24. If conditions are propitious, they are

    uncertain   in favor of
    poor   a hindrance to.

the front area

25. On a stage, the proscenium is probably

    the front area   the balcony
    a side area   the back area.

protrude

26. If *intrude* means literally "to thrust in," what word probably means "to thrust or jut forward"?

proctor

27. Of course not all words beginning with *p, r, o* have the prefix *pro-*. Which one of the following probably does not contain it?

    proctor   pronounce
    proscribe   promise

forward or *for*

28. To reiterate: the prefix *pro-* commonly means "f_____" or "___."

10

NON

1. *Non-* is another negative prefix. Compare the words *non-American* and *un-American*. Which one is *less* emphatic and *less* offensive?

    ___ _____   non-American

2. A glance at the words *non-Christian, noncentral, non-Arab,* and *nonacid* suggests that a hyphen is generally used when the base word begins with a _____ letter.   capital

3. If the *o* in the prefix *non-* is pronounced like the *o* in the word *on*, which of the following pronunciations is correct?   non-English

    non-English
    nun-English

pro*nunciation*

4. If the prefix *non-* is pronounced "non," and the word *none* is pronounced "nun," the way to tell *non-Christian* from *none Christian,* when listening, is to note the difference in pro_____.

non

5. Should the first three letters of *nonconductor* be pronounced "non" or "nun"? ___

*non*fireproof

6. *Non-* is often added to a regular word to give us the negative. If a building is "not fireproof," it is, in a word, ___fireproof.

nonathletic

7. If I am "not athletic," I am _____.

*non*age

8. If I am "not of age" to do certain things, such as marry or sign contracts, I am in my ___age.

un*equal*ed

9. If *par* means "equal," *nonpareil* probably means "un_____ed."

number

10. You would expect the word *nonillion* to refer to a
    waterfall
    number
    notebook

mind

11. In law many terms which make useful vocabulary-building aids are borrowed directly from Latin. Take the phrase *non compos mentis.* Our word *mental* is derived from *mentis,* which you would infer means ____ (rhymes with *find*).

compos*ed*

12. Adding a two-letter past tense ending to *compos* gives you the English word *compos*___.

13. If a person's mind is literally not composed or not put together—*non compos mentis*—he is probably mentally

    unbalanced
    alert
    without compare.

    unbalanced

14. In logic the term *non sequitur* is applied to a conclusion that does ___ follow from the preceding argument.

    not

15. If your ego is your self, anything or everything that is "not" the self is ___ego.

    *non*ego

16. The word that means "no entity" is _____.

    nonentity

17. The opposite of *minus* is the word _____.

    plus

18. When we are "not" able to go, speak, or act further or more, we can be said to be completely ___-plussed.

    *non*plussed

19. If the Latin word-element *chal* means "to care," the English word meaning "not caring" or "indifferent" would be _____*ant*.

    *nonchal*ant

20. A substance having "no" nitrogen would be called _____enous.

    *nonnitrog*enous

21. If a person has no distinguishing features or characteristics, if there is literally nothing to describe or "write down" about him, he is non__script.

    non*de*script

nonresident

22. A person who is not a resident of a country is a
_____.

not

23. As you can see, the prefix *non-*, meaning "___," is
relatively easy to manage.

Verbal Analogy Review Test

Verbal analogies are, to be sure, measures of vocabulary. But that is not all. The fact that they are also found in intelligence tests is a reminder that they also measure your ability to reason, to note relationships between words and ideas — abilities that demand intelligence. No wonder they deserve special attention.

The few analogy items you have tried so far have been connected by words, as in the following example:

Day *is to* night *as* sun *is to* _____.

In mathematics such relationships are expressed as ratio and proportion problems, with symbols substituted for words:

Day : night : : sun : (moon).

You should become acquainted with as many of the relationships as possible so you can handle verbal analogy items more effectively. One such relationship is the common synonym. Another is the antonym. Do the following items to get better acquainted with these patterns as well as to review some of the word parts studied.

1. Proceed : go forward : : recede : go _____.

2. Stupid : clever : : Christian : ___-Christian.

3. Thrust in : intrude : : thrust forward : ___trude.

4. Soft : hard : : add : __duct.

5. *Re-* : back : : *trans-* : _____.

It helps to put the first two words together in a way that makes their relationship obvious: *soft* is the antonym of *hard,* just as *add* is the antonym of _____. Or *proceed* means *go forward,* as *recede* means go _____. Definitions are like synonyms; they are alike in meaning.

Review Test II

A. In the blank after each prefix in the left-hand column, write the number, from the right-hand list, of the common meaning of the prefix. The same meaning may apply to more than one prefix. Some meanings will not be used at all.

1. *un-*	_____	1. forward, for
2. *re-*	_____	2. back, again
		3. in, into
3. *trans-*	_____	4. upper
		5. not
4. *pro-*	_____	6. against
		7. across, beyond
5. *non-*	_____	8. one

B. In each of the following sets of words, there is one word that does *not* contain the prefix found in the rest of the words in that set. Using the principles in Unit 2, find that word and enter the appropriate number in the blank at the right.

1. (1) untied; (2) united; (3) unequal; (4) unwary   1. _____

2. (1) reactor; (2) reason; (3) receive; (4) recess   2. _____

3. (1) transfuse; (2) transcend; (3) translate; (4) tramway   3. _____

4. (1) proclaim; (2) process; (3) probe; (4) profuse   4. _____

5. (1) nonprofit; (2) nonentity; (3) nonce; (4) nonfatal   5. _____

C. Note the phrase in quotation marks in each sentence and express the same idea with a word containing one of the five prefixes in section A.

1. In a word, if a person is "not collegiate" he is _____ .

2. If a person is "moving forward" he is making _____ .

3. If a person is making a flight "across the Atlantic," he is making a _____ flight.

4. If a person is doing something which is "not expected," he is doing an _____ act.

5. If a person "calls something back," he _____ it.

(Answers on page 256.)

Verbal Analogy Review Test

In addition to the similarity, synonym or like-is-to-like, relationships and the dissimilarity, or antonym, relationships, what others should you know? The following five are also important.

1. PART is to WHOLE or ONE is to MANY relationship (sleeve : shirt)
2. PART is to PART relationship (punctuation : spelling)
3. ACTION is to OBJECT relationship (kick : football)
4. OBJECT is to ACTION relationship (steak : broil)
5. CAUSE and EFFECT relationship (sprint : fatigue)

While you're getting better acquainted with each of these five new relationships, why not also get added experience with another type of analogy item, one that gives you a choice between pairs of words.

Here are the directions. From the four pairs of words which follow each initial pairing, select the pair which is related in the same way as the words of the first pair. Always try to figure out the precise relationship of the first two words as accurately as possible. Try the following examples.

1. SLEEVE : SHIRT ::   (1) sea : fish; (2) salad : dinner; (3) gill : fin; (4) instrument : violin.   1. _____

2. PUNCTUATION : SPELLING :: (1) sleeping
   pill : fatigue; (2) after-shave : shaving; 3) bandaid :
   cut; (4) biology : chemistry.   2. _____

3. KICK : FOOTBALL :: (1) kill : gun; (2) break :
   pieces; (3) ask : reply; (4) smoke : cigarette.   3. _____

4. STEAK : BROIL :: (1) bread : bake; (2) food :
   buy; (3) wine : chill; (4) sugar : stir.   4. _____

5. SPRINT : FATIGUE :: (1) track : runner; (2)
   spider : bug; (3) fast : hunger; (4) skiing : walking. 5. _____

If you phrase the relationship between the first two words in item
1 by saying, "A *sleeve* is part of a *shirt*," you make it much easier to
select the answer. Is a *sea* part of a *fish*? Is a *salad* part of a *dinner*? Is a
gill part of a *fin*? Is an *instrument* part of a *violin*? The right answer
stands out nicely: a salad is part of a whole dinner.

If you say *punctuation* and *spelling* are parts or elements of writing,
you'll arrive at *biology* and *chemistry* as parts or subjects in the field of
science, the part-to-part relationship.

If you show the relationship between the first two words in the
third item by the phrase, "You *kick* a *football*," then you are well on
your way to making an easy choice. Do you *kill* a *gun*, *break* a *pieces*,
ask a *reply*? Or do you *smoke* a *cigarette*? Yes, the cigarette is acted upon.

Suppose you phrase the relationship of the next item in this way:
"*Steak* is something you *broil*." That phrasing will not be much help
because *bread* is something you *bake*, *food* is something you *buy*, *wine*
is something you *chill*, *sugar* is something you *stir*. You must look more
closely at the first pair and add a qualifier: "Steak is something you
broil *with heat*." Now you can easily select the right answer. Heat is
needed only in baking bread—the right choice—something you bake.

Finally, *sprinting* causes you to become *fatigued*, just as *fasting*
causes you to become *hungry*—the cause-effect relationship. All these
relationships should be clearer by now, thanks to this added experience.
And tests of this kind should be more easily handled, a matter of practical importance.

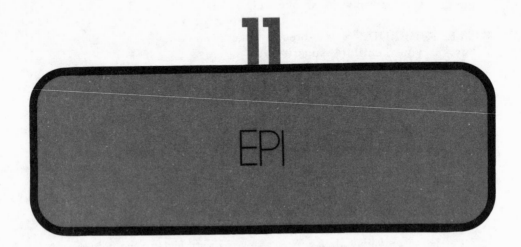

11

EPI

1. When *mono-* is added to axial, you get *monaxial.* (Watch that vowel.) In like manner, when you add *epi-* to *axial* you should get _____.

epaxial

2. One variant spelling or form of *epi-* is apparently __.

ep-

3. Both *mono-* and *epi-* end, not with a consonant, but with a _____.

vowel

4. Both *mono-* and *epi-* are prefixes, not of one syllable, but of ___.

two

5. To generalize, prefixes of two syllables ending in a vowel drop their final vowel when they are added to a root beginning with a _____.

vowel

6. When *mono-* is added to *carp*, you get *monocarp*, a plant that yields fruit only once before dying. In like manner, when you add *epi-* to *carp* you should get _____.

epicarp

7. If you know that the epidermis is the outer layer of your skin, you would expect *epi-* to mean
under
middle
over.

over

8. Yes, *epi-* means "on," "upon," "over," or "on the outside." An inscription "upon" a tomb (*taphos*) is rightly called an ____taph.

*epi*taph

9. A descriptive word or phrase "upon" some person or thing, as "hard-hearted pal," is called an ____thet.

*epi*thet

10. A terse, witty statement "upon" some matter is called an ____gram.

*epi*gram

11. The Greek word *demos*, meaning "people," gives us our word *democracy*. A rapidly spreading disease, literally "upon the people," is called an epi____ic.

epi*demic*

12. If a syn*onym* is a word with the same meaning as another word, and an ant*onym*, a word with an opposite meaning, the Greek word *onyma* probably means
name
person
book.

name

13. If you add *epi-* to *onym*, you should get _____, literally, "named on or over."

eponym

eponym

14. Since Pennsylvania is named after William Penn (*Penn* coming "over" into *Pennsylvania*), *Penn* is the __onym of *Pennsylvania*.

*Elizabeth*an

15. Queen Elizabeth is the eponym of the _____-an period or age.

epitome

16. The Greeks called the smallest particle an *atom*, meaning "not cut or divisible." Substitute *epi-* for *a-*, add an *e* at the end of the root, and you have the word _____.

the abridged version

17. With a book or article you can have a complete or a cut, or abridged, version. Would *epitome*, literally "cut on," refer to the complete or the abridged version? _____

essence

18. *Epitome* has still another common meaning. In the sentence, "I am the very epitome of health," it apparently means
    opposite
    essence
    enemy.

heart

19. The Greek word *kardia*, as in *cardiogram* or *cardiograph*, apparently refers to what part of your anatomy?

on

20. The word *epicardium*, then, apparently refers to a layer of tissue __ or around the heart.

rind

21. The part of an apple that would most appropriately be called the *epicarp* is the
    pulp   stem
    seed   rind
            core.

22. The epicenter of an earthquake would be
    above the place of focus
    in the very middle.   above the place
                                                                     of focus

23. The Greek word *phyte* means "plant." A geophyte
    would, therefore, be an earth _____.   plant

24. If *hydrophobia* is an abnormal fear of water, a plant
    growing only in water would probably be called a
    _____phyte.   *hydro*phyte

25. If the neoclassical period is the new classical period,
    a new plant would rightly be called a ____phyte.   *neo*phyte

26. A "new" convert or member, or a novice, is also
    a ____phyte.   *neo*phyte

27. A plant that grows "upon" another plant but gets
    nourishment from the air, as certain mosses, is
    called an ____phyte—an "upon" plant.   *epi*phyte

28. The meanings "on," "upon," "over," or "on the
    outside" should now be firmly linked to the pre-
    fix ____.   epi-

12

MIS

*mis*plays

1. The prefix *mis-* means "wrong" or "wrongly." If one "plays" a wrong card he ___plays.

misfires

2. Or if, in an engine, a cylinder does not "fire" properly, we say it _____.

misfit

3. If a dress is too large or small and does not "fit" properly, we could call it a _____.

mis-

4. Watch for possible confusion between *miso-* meaning "to hate" and the prefix ___, meaning "wrong" or "wrongly."

*miso*gamist

5. If *gamos* is a Greek word meaning "marriage," someone who "hates marriage" would be a _____-gamist, not a misgamist.

6. If *gynist* comes from the Greek *gyne*, meaning "woman," a "woman hater" would be a _____-_____.

    misogynist

7. If you remember that *neo-* is a combining form meaning "new," you would infer that *misoneism* would mean hatred of ___ things.

    new

8. What closely related word would mean "one who hates new things"?
    misoneism
    misoneist
    misoneology

    misoneist

9. You drop the final *o* in *mono-* when you add it to a root beginning with a vowel, as in *monaxial*. From this, you could infer that *miso-* added to *anthrope* would give you _____.

    misanthrope

10. Always look after the *s*. If *mis-* is followed by a vowel other than *o*, there is reason to suspect the *shortened* form of _____, meaning "hate."

    miso-

11. If you quote incorrectly or wrongly, you _____.

    misquote

12. A printing error is usually spoken of as a _____.

    misprint

13. If you put or place something in the "wrong" place, you are said to _____ it.

    misplace

14. The Latin word *nomen* means "name." At a meeting when you propose someone as an officer, you are said to name, or _____ate, him.

    *nomin*ate

15. Drop the *en* from *nomen* and add *de plume* and you have *nom de plume*, the French phrase for pen _____.

pen *name*

16. You would infer that a *misnomer* would be a _____ name for something.

wrong

17. To inform someone "wrongly" would be to ___-_____.

misinform

18. In *misinform*, the vowel following the *mis-* suggests the possibility of *miso-* in shortened form. A check of meaning, however, shows no idea of the meaning of *miso-*, which is _____.

hate

19. If a book is "wrongly translated" it is _____-_____.

mistranslated

20. If a book is "not" translated it is __translated.

*un*translated

21. If something is represented "wrongly" it is ___-_____.

misrepresented

22. An error can also be called a _____.

mistake

23. If money is not used correctly, it is _____.

misused

24. If an actor or actress is "cast" in an unsuitable role, that person is _____.

miscast

25. Prefix knowledge is an aid to spelling also. Always keep the *s* when adding *mis-* to a word. With this in mind, which of the following is spelled correctly?
mishape
misshape

misshape

26. Now you need not "spell" a word the "wrong" way
and worry about _____ in your letters.   misspellings

27. The prefix *mis-* should now bring to mind the
meanings "w____" or "_____ly."   *wrong, wrong*ly

13

OB

1. As you know, an obnoxious person is
   sleepy
   objectionable
   suspicious.

objectionable

2. When you know that *noxious* comes from a Latin word, you should also know that *obnoxious* contains the prefix

   o-   *obn-*
   ob-   *obno-*.

ob-

3. Usually an obstinate person is not *for* a change but a_____ it.

against

4. Similarly, an obstacle is something that does not facilitate your forward progress but works _____ it.

against

96

5. Apparently, a common meaning of the prefix *ob-* is
   behind   beside
   against   far.

   against

6. For another meaning of *ob-*, think of *objective*.
   When you have a goal or objective, do you try to go
   "to or toward" it or "away" from it?

   to or toward

7. "To or toward" is apparently another common
   meaning of the prefix __.

   ob-

8. Now for the most important principle of all in dealing with prefixes. In the word *assimilate*, the second
   and third letters are
   different
   alike.

   alike

9. One meaning of *assimilate* is "to make like." If one
   culture is assimilated by another, it is made ____
   the other culture.

   like

10. When one letter is _____ by another, it is
    made like it.

    assimilated

11. Why this change? Which of the following is an
    easier combination of letters to pronounce?
    obpress
    oppress

    oppress

12. When *ob-* is added to *press*, the *b* in *ob-* is assimi-
    lated, or made like the letter _ in *press*.

    p

13. Judging from the word *occlude*, before roots begin-
    ning with *c*, you would expect the *b* in *ob-* to as-
    similate to a _.

    c

f

14. If *offer* also contains an assimilated form of *ob-*, before roots beginning with an *f* you would expect the *b* in *ob-* to become an __.

ob-

15. Now you know that *op-*, *oc-*, and *of-* are all assimilated forms of the prefix ___.

*o*mit

16. However, you should note that when you add *ob-* to *mit*, you drop the *b* completely, to make the word __*mit*.

m

17. Judging from this example, you drop the final *b* only when adding *ob-* to a root beginning with the letter __.

third

18. To aid in spotting assimilative changes, remember *oppress*, *occlude*, and *offer*. In each of the three words the second and _____ letters are identical.

prefix

19. The sign of the doubled consonant, as in *offer*, *assimilate*, and *effort*, suggests the presence of an assimilated form of some _____.

against

20. Remembering a common meaning of *ob-*, you would define an opponent as one who is playing _____ you, not for you.

*ob*stinate

21. Some people are agreeable. Others are fixed and unyielding and can be called __stinate.

unruly

22. If a horse is obstreperous, the prefix suggests he is
    quiet
    slow
    unruly.

23. Your prefix knowledge should help you define the word *objurgate* as to
    sing loudly
    denounce strongly
    praise highly.

    denounce
    strongly

24. With principles of assimilation in mind, which of the following words does not contain the prefix *ob-* in any of its variant forms?
    occur   offend
    ocellus   opprobrium

    ocellus

25. Prefix knowledge should suggest that a speech of obloquy would be a speech of
    censorship
    greeting
    farewell.

    censorship

26. If a man is obsessed by some fixed idea, that obsession works _____ his having a well-rounded personality.

    against

27. Do not forget assimilative principles when you write the antonym of *defensive*, which is _____

    offensive

28. *To obfuscate*, judging from the prefix, is
    to state   to explain
    to encourage   to confuse.

    to confuse

29. Using prefix meaning, the word *oppugn* probably means
    open   cooperate
    assail   succeed.

    assail

30. As a review, remember that "against," "to", or "toward" are the common meanings of the prefix __.

    ob-

31. Remember also the principle of assimilation, which most commonly means that the last letter in the prefix is changed to be the same as the first letter in the r___ which follows, when the letter in question is a consonant.

root

Verbal Analogy Review Test

There are still more common relationships that need to be explored, if you are to feel comfortably at home with the analogy test item. And there's still another popular form for such items that you should know. Here are the new relationships and test forms.

First, look at these new relationships.

1. Purpose relationship (as *glove : ball*)
2. Place relationship (as *stove : kitchen*)
3. Degree relationship (as *warm : hot*)
4. Characteristic or association relationship (as *Satan : wrong*)
5. Sequence relationship (as *fall : winter*)

Keep those five relationships in mind as you try a new form of test item. With these you are given the first three elements in the relationship. You provide the last word to complete the analogy. For example: *Day* is to *night* as *cold* is to _____ 1) summer; 2) hot; 3) cool; 4) wet. With *day and night* as opposites, you should choose *hot*, the opposite of *cold*. The following items illustrate the five relationships mentioned above.

1. GLOVE : BALL :: HOOK :   (1) line; (2) fish; (3) bait; (4) boat.

    1. _____

2. STOVE : KITCHEN :: BATHTUB :   (1) bedroom; (2) basement; (3) garage; (4) bathroom; (5) kitchen.

    2. _____

3. WARM : HOT :: WATER :   (1) wet; (2) soap; (3) steam; (4) heat.

    3. _____

4. SATAN : WRONG :: ICE :   (1) water; (2) cold; (3) clear; (4) drink; (5) heat.

    4. _____

5. FALL : WINTER :: WEDNESDAY :   (1) Friday; (2) Tuesday; (3) Thursday; (4) Sunday; (5) spring.

5. _____

Again, observe the precise relationships between the first two words. They provide the basis for accurate choice of the remaining word. For example, you use a *glove* for the purpose of catching a *ball*. By the same token, you use a *hook* for the purpose of catching what—a *line*, a *fish*, a *bait*, or a *boat*? Your phrasing of the relationship should help to make the right answer stand out.

Generally speaking, a *stove* belongs in the *kitchen*, as a *bathtub* belongs in the *bathroom*. *Warm* and *hot* are degrees of temperature just as *water* and *steam* reflect different degrees of temperature. *Satan* is associated with *wrong*, just as *ice* is associated with *cold* more strongly than with *clear* or *water*. Since *fall* is followed by *winter*, you would expect *Wednesday* to be followed by *Thursday* to show the same relationship.

Once you get acquainted with such common relationship patterns, you will manage the analogy tests much more easily—far better than those not knowing what possible relationships to look for.

14

EX

1. If *exclude* means "to keep someone out," and an exile is one who is turned out of the country, *ex-* apparently means "___."

out

2. "Beyond" is still another meaning of *ex-*. When you are excessively tired, you are not weary in an average way, but are tired b_____ the average.

beyond

3. In the words *expel* and *eject*, the prefix meaning that seems uppermost is
out
beyond.

out

4. The meaning "former" or "previous" is still an-

other to be noted. In which of the following words
does this meaning appear?

exhale

extreme

ex-wife

ex-wife

5. When the prefix *ex-* means "former" or "previous,"
it is usually joined by a hyphen to the second part
of the word. Therefore, would the word for "former convict" be written *ex-convict* or *exconvict?*

_____

ex-convict

6. There is possible confusion between the Greek prefixes *exo-* and *ecto-* and the prefix __, meaning
"out."

ex-

7. Fortunately both *exo-* and *ecto-* have the same common meaning as *ex-*, the meaning "___."

out

8. *Ex-* has a few assimilated forms to watch out for.
Just as *ob-* added to *fer* resulted in *offer*, so *ex-* added
to *fort* gives us _____.

effort

9. Just as *ob-* becomes *o-* before *mit*, to make *omit*, so
ex- before *mit* becomes _.

e- (emit)

10. The final *x*, however, is dropped not only before *m*
but also before *b*, *d*, *g*, *l*, *n*, *r*, and *v*. Which of the
following is correct?

elect

ellect

exlect

elect

11. Use a pronunciation rule of thumb to help determine what form is most likely when prefix and root

evolve

elements are joined. For example, which is easier to pronounce — exvolve or evolve? _____

eccentric
escape

12. With a very few words, the *ex-* is assimilated to *ec-* or *es-*, as in __*centric* and __*cape*.

ex-

13. Be on the alert for an *e-*, *ef-*, *ec-*, or *es-*, all variant or assimilative forms of the prefix __.

*ex*hausted

14. When you are completely worn "out," we can say you are __hausted.

*ex*tinguishing

15. A fireman can distinguish himself by putting "out" a fire or ex_____ it.

out

16. When you efface all traces of some action, you wipe ___ all traces of it.

*ef*fects

17. Out of causes you have the inevitable __fects.

extern

18. If an intern lives "in" a hospital as a resident doctor, a doctor who is affiliated with a hospital, but lives "outside" it, is called an _____.

*ex*tracted

19. If one of your teeth is pulled "out," we say it's been ex_____.

efflux

20. Remembering the principles of assimilation, if an influx is a "flowing in," a "flowing out" would be called an _____.

erupt

21. If *rupt* comes from a Latin word meaning "to break," "to break out," as lava from a volcano, would be to _____.

22. When everyone is pulled out of a besieged or threatened city, they are _vacuated.

*ev*acuated

23. If, through court action, a landlord puts a tenant "out," he is said to _vict him.

*ev*ict

24. When you put "out" some energy to do some work, you __ert yourself.

*ex*ert

25. Your knowledge of prefixes should suggest that if a book is expurgated, parts of it are

added   poorly written
removed   rewritten.

removed

26. Use your knowledge of prefixes to define *expatiate*. It probably means

to conserve
to threaten
to enlarge.

to enlarge

27. You would expect *exogamy* to mean marriage

with an older person
outside the tribe or clan
between relatives.

outside the tribe
or clan

28. Now whenever you see the prefix *ex-*, remember the meanings "___," "beyond," "former," or "previous."

out

As further review, apply your knowledge of *ex-* in the following test. Since some three thousand new words edge their way into our language every year, it pays to know the indispensable shortcuts. *Over a thousand words* of a desk-sized dictionary, for example, contain a form of *ex-*. You can be sure that many new words will make use of that old element also.

1. If you saw an *egress*, what should you do? (1) shoot
   it; (2) photograph it; (3) go out; (4) hop on board.

   1. _____

2. *Elide* means (1) play; (2) add; (3) sew; (4) leave out.

   2. _____

3. *Ebullient* means (1) bubbling; (2) durable; (3) bulb-
   shaped; (4) quiet.

   3. _____

4. *Excaudate* means (1) buried; (2) without tail; (3)
   short; (4) full of dirt.

   4. _____

5. *Eclectic* means (1) eulogistic; (2) poetic; (3) dis-
   eased; (4) selective.

   5. _____

When you progress, you go forward; when you regress,
you go back. When you *egress*, you go "out." When you
pronounce *February*, you should not elide or leave
"out" the first *r*. Her ebullient personality marked her
out in any group; she bubbled "out" with *ex*citement
and enthusiasm. *Excaudate* names the species without
any tail—*ex-* (out) + *caudate* (tail). An eclectic approach is one that takes the best "out" of several ap-
proaches. Since you select from several sources, you
are selective.

Verbal Analogy Review Test

One last group of relationships will be introduced, making a total
of seventeen fairly common relationships to be noted. That is not an
exhaustive list but should cover most of the relationships found on the
usual scholarship and aptitude tests you are likely to take. Experience with these seventeen should suggest still others that you can handle because of your practice.

Still another form of the analogy test will be used, the third type
you will be likely to meet. It is used in the Miller Analogy Test, considered by many as the most reliable and valid test available for selecting graduate students in universities and high-level personnel in
business, industry, and government. People being considered for mana-
gerial or supervisory roles may well find themselves judged by this test.

With this form either of the last two words must be provided. Regardless of position, you must select the choice which completes the relationship with the other three words. An example will let you see how the items are structured.

SUBMARINE : FISH ::   (1) kite; (2) canoe; (3) feather;
(4) chirp : bird.

Since you'll find *submarines* and *fish* in the water, you'll select *kite* as the right answer. You'll find a *kite* and a *bird* in the air, ordinarily.

Here are the last five relationships to examine:

1. Person-Specialty relationship (podiatrist : feet)
2. Young-Old and Small-Large relationships (colt : horse)
3. Material-Product relationships (wool : suit)
4. Grammatical relationships (return : climb—both verbs)
5. Identical prefix, root, or suffix relationships (cooperate : collaborate—both with identical prefix and suffix)

Now try the following five items, illustrating further the relationships just introduced.

1. PODIATRIST : FEET ::   (1) lexicographer; (2) optometrist; (3) jurist; (4) conductor : DICTIONARY.   1. _____

2. COLT : HORSE ::   (1) lioness; (2) yearling; (3) vixen; (4) cub : LION.   2. _____

3. WOOL : SUIT :: LEATHER :   (1) shirt; (2) shoes; (3) soap; (4) table.   3. _____

4. RETURN : CLIMB :: STUDY :   (1) give; (2) friend; (3) studious; (4) large.   4. _____

5. COOPERATE : COLLABORATE :: SUBDUE : (1) collide; (2) support; (3) arise; (4) work; (5) terminate.   5. _____

A *podiatrist's* specialty is *feet*, just as a *lexicographer's* is the *dictionary*. A *colt* is a young *horse*, just as a lion *cub* is a young *lion*. You use material called *wool* to make a *suit;* you use material called *leather* to make *shoes*. Both *return* and *climb* are verbs. Both *give* and *study* are verbs, *friend* being a noun and *studious* and *large* being adjectives. Finally, both *cooperate* and *collaborate* contain a form of the prefix *com-* and the suffix *-ate*. There are no two words with the same suffix in the last pair, but both *subdue* and *support* contain a form of the prefix *sub-*. That makes *support* the right answer.

At this point you've been introduced to a total of seventeen of the most common relationships found in verbal analogy tests. Since this type of test is so widely used, it pays you to develop skill and sureness in handling such items. In addition you've familiarized yourself with the usual forms used for this type of test.

In these days when schools have been criticized for declining test scores in writing and reading, you can have the satisfaction of knowing that you are for yourself turning the tide in the other direction. The Scholastic Aptitude Test (SAT) frequently associated with this decline is taken nationwide. The SAT test requires skill and familiarity with tests of opposites, verbal analogies, and sentence completion. By the time you finish this book, you will feel well at home with any and all of these test forms.

15

DIS

1. *Dis-* has only two variant forms or disguises. Just as *ob-* added to *fer* gives *offer*, so *dis-* added to *fer* gives _____.

   differ

2. There is only one other variant besides *dif-* (used only before *f*). Just as *ex-* added to *vict* gives *evict*, so *dis-* added to *vert* should give _____.

   divert

3. Generally, before roots beginning with *b, d, g, v, m, n, l,* and *r,* the *s* in *dis-* is dropped completely. *Dis-* plus *late* should normally give you _____.

   dilate

4. From now on, watch for *dif-* and *di-*, the only two assimilated forms of the prefix ____.

   dis-

not

5. One meaning of *dis-* is "not," as in the word *dis-honest*, or ____ honest.

apart or away

6. In addition to its negative meaning, *dis-* also means "separation," as in *dismiss* and *disperse* where *dis-* means
with or together
apart or away
down.

apart

7. Thus in a laboratory when an animal is dissected for study it is cut a _____.

away

8. When someone distributes handbills to pedestrians, he does not keep them but gives them _____.

dis-

9. Beware of possible confusion between *di-*, a prefix meaning "two," and *di-*, a variant form of the prefix ____.

two

10. If a *dilemma* is defined as "a choice between equally disagreeable alternatives," the presence of *di-*, meaning "____," is suggested.

apart

11. With some words, meaning will not help, as with *divide*. If you divide an apple you may cut it in "two" or cut it a_____.

divulge

12. *Vulge* comes from a Latin word meaning "common people." What word probably means to make known to the people or to "part" with some information? _____

discord

13. The opposite of *honest* is *dishonest*. The opposite of *harmony* is *disharmony* or ____*cord*.

14. To persuade is to get someone to do or believe something. The word ___*suade* probably means to turn someone "away" from a course of action.

    *dis*suade

15. In a hotel, if you wish to sleep in the morning, just hang a sign on the door, "Do not _____."

    disturb

16. When an army officer sends a message "away," the officer is said to ___*patch* it.

    *dis*patch

17. If the Latin verb *sociare* means "to join," the word meaning to "sever associations" would be to _____ yourself.

    disassociate

18. If *sipate* comes from a Latin word meaning "to throw," a man who throws or wastes "away" his energies and substance could be said to _____ them.

    dissipate

19. If a bear lodged in a tree is driven "away," it is _____.

    dislodged

20. When you leave on board a ship, you embark on a trip. When you return and land, you do not embark, you _____.

    disembark

21. Your knowledge of prefixes lets you know that when money is disbursed it is
    parted with   saved
    accepted   counted.

    parted with

22. Judging from the prefix, the noun *dishabille* probably means
    informally dressed   completely dressed
    formally attired   partially dressed.

    partially dressed

not alike

23. Disparate elements are probably

quite similar   heavy
hopeless   not alike.

dislike

24. When there is no middle ground, you either like something or _____ it.

disillusion

25. The reverse of *illusion* is *"not"* *illusion* or ___- _____.

divorce

26. If a married couple decides to part and go separate ways, they usually get a _____.

not

27. The two meanings of *dis-* to keep in mind are "___" and "part" or "away."

The more experience you have in word analysis and in applying your newly acquired knowledge of prefix meaning, the more useful this approach becomes. Keep the meanings "away" and "not" in mind as you try to deal with the following difficult words.

1. _____

1. If you're *diffident,* you're   (1) quarrelsome; (2) shy; (3) friendly; (4) careful.

2. _____

2. If you *disparage* something, you   (1) rearrange it; (2) extol it; (3) replace it; (4) belittle it.

3. _____

3. *Discursive* means   (1) speaking; (2) scholarly; (3) deserving; (4) wandering.

4. _____

4. *Distrain* means   (1) to draw tight; (2) to pretend; (3) to travel; (4) to take something away.

5. _____

5. *Discommode* means   (1) serve; (2) oppose; (3) disturb; (4) supply.

If a person is diffident, he tends to stay "away" from the center of things—to withdraw. The dictionary tells us that diffident comes from *dis* + *fidere* (to trust). When we have no trust in ourselves, we are shy or diffident. Add *com-* to *fidere* and you have to "trust together," or *confidence*. Obviously increasing your word power means more confidence and less diffidence. If something is disparaged, it is belittled—something is taken "away" from it. A discursive account tends to wander "away" from the point. Distrain is a legal term for describing the seizing of property as security for some debt. In short, you take "away" some property until the claim is settled, a move which may discommode the owner and take "away" from his peace of mind.

Review Test III

A. In the blank after each prefix in the left-hand column, write the number, from the right-hand list, of the common meaning of the prefix. The same meaning may apply to more than one prefix. Some meanings will not be used at all.

1. *epi-*	_____	1. apart, not
		2. above
2. *mis-*	_____	3. out, beyond
		4. wrong
3. *ob-*	_____	5. within
		6. upon
4. *ex-*	_____	7. against
		8. near, by
5. *dis-*	_____	

B. In each of the following sets of words, there is one word that does *not* contain the prefix found in the rest of the words in that set. Using the principles in Unit 2, find that word and enter the appropriate number in the blank at right.

1. (1) epigram; (2) epicritic; (3) epilogue; (4) epic   1. _____

2. (1) misinform; (2) misery; (3) misstatement; (4) mis-
   cue   2. _____

3. (1) obsolete; (2) obelisk; (3) offend; (4) occlude; (5)
   oppress   3. _____

4. (1) exit; (2) egress; (3) efflux; (4) extrabold   4. _____

5. (1) dismiss; (2) disjunctive; (3) diffuse; (4) divert; (5)
   digitate   5. _____

C. Use your knowledge of prefixes to help you deal with the relatively
   strange words in the following vocabulary test. Enter the appropriate number in the blank at the right.

1. *Eparch* means   (1) old person; (2) ruler over a pro-
   vince; (3) loyal individual; (4) citizen.   1. _____

2. *Misfeasance* means   (1) surface; (2) substitute; (3)
   spokesman; (4) wrongdoing.   2. _____

3. *Objurgate* means   (1) speak against; (2) agree with;
   (3) judge; (4) juggle.   3. _____

4. *Effete* means   (1) feminine; (2) courageous; (3)
   worn out; (4) difficult.   4. _____

5. *Disburse* means   (1) pay out; (2) take in; (3) burden;
   (4) improve.   5. _____

(*Answers on page 256.*)

Sentence Completion Review Test

Still another common type of vocabulary test item is sentence
completion. With these you lean heavily on context. In a sense such
items effectively measure your skill with context, your mental agility,
and your verbal accuracy. You have to look for implications, for contextual clues of a variety of kinds, in order to fill in the blanks accurately.

Directions for such test items are as follows. Select from the words
given the one that best fits the meaning of the sentence. Read the

choices carefully, weighing the various clues, including word-part meanings, before making your choice. Try this sample item — this paradigm:

> If you take a gloomy view of things you should be called
> a   (1) liar; (2) neophyte; (3) realist; (4) pessimist.

The dictionary defines a pessimist as one who tends "to take the gloomiest possible view of a situation."

The following items will provide added experience and added review of words and word parts.

Be sure you note prefix meanings as you work through such tests. For example, in item 6, you have the word *re*stitution, with the prefix *re-*, meaning "back or again." If the criminal gave "back" what he had stolen, that might explain the leniency. Even if you're not certain what *restitution* means, you should know *re-*. Use that knowledge to advantage. (Answers are on page 256.)

1. An _____ is something which spreads rapidly and extensively among people in an area.
   (1) illness; (2) ideal; (3) epidemic; (4) exorcism; (5) addition

   1. _____

2. A _____ is one who hates or distrusts mankind.
   (1) misanthrope; (2) polemic; (3) benefactor; (4) tycoon; (5) tyrant.

   2. _____

3. The custom of marrying outside the tribe, family, clan, or other social unit is called _____.
   (1) endogamy; (2) exogamy; (3) bigamy; (4) monogamy

   3. _____

4. His use of big words confused everyone, and instead of clarifying the issues, he only _____ them.
   (1) amplified; (2) refuted; (3) obfuscated; (4) elucidated; (5) iterated

   4. _____

5. Almost everyone agreed. Only a few _____ opinions were voiced.
   (1) constructive; (2) inexorable; (3) vaunted; (4) magnanimous; (5) dissident

   5. _____

6. Since the criminal made _____ for the stolen goods, the judge showed leniency.
   (1) restitution; (2) exigency; (3) allegiance; (4) gestures; (5) transmigrations

   6. _____

7. When public officers serve solely for the benefit of the people, no person has any more _____ right than another to hold office.
   (1) sincere; (2) technical; (3) confidential; (4) subversive; (5) intrinsic

   7. _____

8. Publication of the book was timed to _____ with the professor's sixtieth birthday.
   (1) terminate; (2) amalgamate; (3) coincide; (4) harmonize; (5) retrogress

   8. _____

9. Someone who claims or demands a place of special merit without really deserving it is said to be _____.
   (1) retentive; (2) extenuating; (3) senile; (4) sedentary; (5) pretentious

   9. _____

10. _____ remarks are those which have no order or connection.
    (1) Incoherent; (2) Puissant; (3) Irrelevant; (4) Ruminative; (5) Abysmal

    10. _____

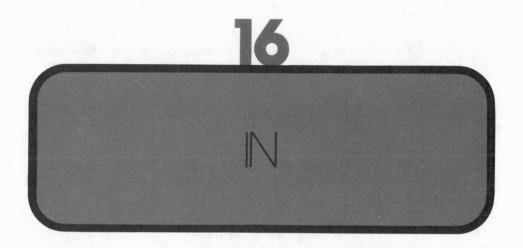

16

IN

1. If *insecure* means "not secure" and *insane* means "not sane," you would infer that *in-* means "___."

   not

2. *In-*, however, has an identical twin which must be remembered. One *in-* means "in" or "into," the other means "___."

   not

3. *To assimilate* is "to make similar or like." When *in-* is added to *literate*, the *n* is assimilated by the *l* to give *__literate* or "not" literate.

   *il*literate

4. When *in-* is added to a root beginning with *r*, you have the same kind of change; *in-* plus *ruption* gives the word _____.

   irruption

5. A labial sound is one made mainly by motion of the

m

lips. Which one of the following letters requires the lips in pronouncing—*l, m, n,* or *t*?

*im*partial

6. Before the labials *m, p,* and *b, in-* becomes *im-,* as in __*partial.*

immortal

7. The ease-of-pronunciation check is useful. Sound each letter distinctly. Which of the following is somewhat easier to pronounce?
   immortal
   inmortal

the first
(*impossible* and *imbalance*)

8. The other labials *p* and *b* have the same effect. Which is easier to pronounce, the first or second in each of these pairs?
   impossible *or* inpossible
   imbalance *or* inbalance

*in*vulnerable

9. This useful negative prefix helps us condense two words into one, to turn, for example, "not vulnerable" into __*vulnerable.*

*invol*untarily

10. The Latin word *volo* means "willing." When we do something unwillingly or accidentally, we may be said to do it _____untarily.

invisible

11. If an object is out of sight and "not" visible, we would call it _____.

invalid

12. If *validus* is a Latin word meaning "strong," one who is not strong but sickly and weak is called an _____.

not

13. If *utilis* is a Latin word meaning "useful," the word *inutile* probably means "___ useful."

14. Our word *urban* as opposed to *rural* is derived from the Latin word *urbs,* which you would infer means
city
country.

city

15. Since city people were thought to be more smooth and polished in manner, the adjective *urbane* came into our language, derived from the Latin word ____, meaning "city."

urbs

16. If you are *inurbane,* you
lack polish   are carefree
are impractical   act on impulse.

lack polish

17. If *trepid* comes from a Latin word meaning "alarmed," you should expect *intrepid* to mean
cowardly   weary
fearless   wise.

fearless

18. If I am "not" tolerant, I am, in a word, _____-_____.

intolerant

19. In which of the following words do you have the prefix *in-,* meaning "not"?
intend   inductive
intemperate   invite

intemperate

20. If something can "not" be suffered, it is _____-_____.

insufferable

21. If *flammable* means "burnable," you might expect *inflammable* to mean "___ burnable."

not

22. But *inflammable* contains the other prefix *in-* and actually means easily set "in" flames or burnable.

in

This suggests the danger of confusing the *in-* meaning "not" with the *in-* meaning "__."

illegal

23. If an act is "not" legal, it is, in a word, _____.

read

24. If *legere* is a Latin word meaning "to read," you would expect legible writing to be writing that could be _____.

illegible

25. If someone's writing is "not" legible or readable, you would call it _____.

*im*measurable

26. If the results are not capable of being measured, you would call them __measurable.

*im*partial

27. If you favor no one side or party more than another, you are indeed a fair and __partial critic.

irrelevant

28. When in a discussion a speaker makes a point that is "not" relevant, we call it an _____ remark.

in-

29. Remember that *il- im-*, and *ir-* may be assimilated forms of the prefix __.

1. To discover what *com-* means, think of words beginning with *com-*, such as *combine, compress,* and ___*pile.*

*com*pile

2. Now look more closely at *combine* and *compress.* If you combine the necessary ingredients to make a cake, you do not keep them separate; you mix them t_____.

together

3. Now you can use other words beginning with *com-* to check the assumption that *com-* means "together." When you compress something into smaller space, you press it more tightly _____.

together

4. You can see that *com-* means "together" or "with." But that knowledge is not as useful as it should be

assimilated

unless you can identify all the as_____ed forms of *com-*.

collision

5. Remember the common meaning of *assimilate* ("to make like"). You would, with that definition in mind, expect *com-* plus *lision* (from *laedere*, "to strike") to result in the word ___*lision*.

correspond

6. Similarly, when adding *com-* to a root beginning with *r*, such as *respond*, you would expect *com-* plus *respond* to lead to ___*respond*.

coeducation

7. Just as with certain other prefixes, the assimilative change is a dropping of the final consonant. When adding *com-* to *education* (a root beginning with a vowel), you get __*education*.

cohere

8. *Com-* also drops its *m* before roots beginning with *h* or *w*, which means *com-* plus *here* gives you __*here*, not *comhere*.

concept

9. Only one other assimilative change exists: the change of *m* to *n* before roots beginning with *c*, *d*, *f*, *g*, *h*, *q*, *s*, *t*, and *v*, as in ___*cept*.

corrode

10. Don't rely on memory. Use the pronunciation rule of thumb — saying the word fast — to bring you to the appropriate change from *comrode* to ___*rode*.

collect

11. Not *conlect* but ___*lect* is correct.

cooperate

12. And not *comoperate* but _____ is correct.

13. If *trahere* means "to draw," the name of a legal

device for drawing two or more parties "together" on some agreement is ___tract.

*con*tract

14. If *nectere* means "to fasten," when you bring two wires "together," you are said to _____ them.

connect

15. If *preempt* means to "buy before," the word which would probably mean to buy the entire supply "together" is __*empt*.

*co*empt

16. If *inherent* means literally "sticking into," the word which probably means "sticking together" is _____.

coherent

17. Now use your prefix knowledge to help you define *collate* as

to compare   to remedy
to read   to delay.

to compare

18. If you "labor with" someone on a writing project, you ___laborate with him.

*col*laborate

19. A *colleague* of yours is probably a

neighbor   manager
fellow worker   stranger.

fellow worker

20. If *bat* is a root derived from the Latin word meaning "to beat or fight," the English word meaning "to fight with" would be _____.

combat

21. If you are asked to serve with others on some project, the group is usually called a ___mittee.

*com*mittee

22. If you remember that *panis* is a Latin word meaning

*com*panion

"bread" and that breaking bread "together" is an ancient rite of friendship, you see where we got the word ___*panion.*

23. The members of a church are sometimes spoken of as a flock, a meaning derived from the Latin *gregare,* "to gather in a flock." That in turn gives us our word _____.

congregation

24. If *progress* is "stepping forward," and *regress,* "stepping back," the word which literally means "stepping together" is _____.

congress

25. If the Latin *sequi* means "to follow," that which follows as a result of something is called a ____-*sequence.*

*con*sequence

26. If the Latin word *tangere* means "to touch," when one person gets in touch "with" another, he is said to _____ that person.

contact

27. Watch for possible confusion between *contra-,* meaning "against," and *con-,* an assimilated form of *com-.* Which one of the following words does not contain a form of *com-?*

contradict

contribute   convention
control   contradict

28. The common meanings of *com-* are "with" or "_____."

together

29. The four variant forms are *col-, con-, cor-,* and __.

co-

For further review, apply your prefix knowledge to the words in the following synonym test.

1. _____

1. If a word is labeled *colloquial* in the dictionary, does that mean it is (1) substandard; (2) vulgar; (3) incorrect; or (4) conversational?

2. _____

2. A *compeer* is (1) a look; (2) an associate; (3) a sightseer; (4) a nobleman.

3. _____

3. *Complot* means (1) conspiracy; (2) criminal; (3) story; (4) garden.

4. _____

4. *Conjugal* means (1) matrimonial; (2) judicial; (3) military; (4) personal.

5. _____

5. *Contiguous* means (1) unfavorable; (2) touching; (3) spreading; (4) angular.

With well over a thousand words of a desk-sized dictionary containing a form of the prefix *com-*, it is a particularly useful shortcut to word meanings. The words *loquacious, eloquent,* and *elocution* are all derived from *loqui,* meaning "to speak," as is true with *colloquial,* literally "to speak together," as in conversation. A colloquialism is, therefore, proper to casual conversation. A compeer is someone we associate "with" on a fairly equal basis. Since conspiracies are usually the work of several people, when you plot "with" someone that becomes a complot. The words *conjugal, junction, juncture, join,* and *conjunction* all have a form of *jungere,* meaning "to join." When two people are joined "together" as man and wife they have a conjugal relationship, a state of matrimony. When two things touch, they are "together," hence contiguous.

18

SUB

1. Since you know that a submarine runs under water, you will have no trouble remembering that *sub-* means "_____."

under

2. While the idea of "under," "beneath," "below" is perhaps the most common meaning, *sub-* also means "lower in rank or position." If there are agents and subagents, the subagents are _____ in rank or position than the agents.

lower

3. Your dictionary mentions still other meanings for the idea of under—such as "to a lesser degree than," "somewhat," "slightly." In which of the following words is that meaning dominant?
subdivided
subhuman

subhuman

4. After learning the meaning, you must learn how to identify *sub-* in actual words. With *sub-*, this means recognizing seven variant forms. Just as *dis-* plus *fer* equals *differ*, so *sub-* plus *fer* would equal ___*fer*.

suffer

5. This change of the last letter in *sub-* to the first letter of the root is most common. For example, before *g* as in *gest*, *sub-* would become ___.

sug-

6. And before *m*, as in *mon*, *sub-* becomes ___.

sum-

7. This same pattern holds when you add *sub-* to *cumb* to get ___*cumb*, to give in or give up under overwhelming pressure.

*succ*umb

8. Try pronouncing the combinations both ways as a further check. Which of the following is easier to say distinctly?
   subplant
   supplant

supplant

9. Before an *r*, as in *render*, *sub-* combines to make ___*render*.

*surr*ender

10. One other somewhat different change occurs: *sub-* sometimes becomes *sus-* before a *p*, *t*, or *c*. Therefore, when you add *sub-* to *pend*, you get ___*pend*, not *suppend*.

*sus*pend

11. From the following words, see if you can pick the one that does not contain the prefix *sub-*.
    supply   supreme
    suspect   surrogate

supreme

sound

12. The third step—the payoff—is using this knowledge effectively in arriving at word meanings. For example, *sonic* comes from a Latin word meaning "sound." When we travel at sonic speed, we travel at the speed of _____.

super*sonic*

13. When a plane passes the sonic barrier, it exceeds the speed of sound or travels at *super* _____ speed.

*sub*sonic

14. Of course, the majority of us still travel at speeds "under" those of sound, or ___*sonic* speeds.

*sub*conscious

15. We are conscious of many things, but some of our mental activity is "under" our conscious level and is therefore called ___conscious.

brought under control

16. When a nation is *subjugated,* the prefix suggests that it is
brought under control
set free
disorganized.

*sub*versive

17. Action designed to overthrow the established order is well described by the word meaning literally "to turn under," a ___*versive* action.

suffer

18. If *fer* comes from *ferre,* meaning "to bear," when pain bears you "under," you are said to _____.

suppress

19. If you impress a friend with the need to keep certain facts "under" cover, you try to _____ those facts.

*sus*pect

20. When you doubt or distrust someone, you tend to look "under" the surface because you ___*pect* him.

21. When the water from a big wave sinks or falls, it is said to ___*side*.

*sub*side

22. When light is diffused it is "poured in every direction." When light is suffused it is overspread—literally, poured _____.

under

23. The last step—to generalize—is a reminder that by studying a few elements carefully we can learn about others also. If *merge* comes from a Latin word meaning "to plunge," our word meaning "to plunge under" would probably be _____.

submerge

24. Now if you remember the prefix meaning "out," you should know that the word meaning "to plunge out" would be _*merge*.

emerge

25. And if you know the prefix meaning "in," you will know that the word meaning "to plunge in" would be __*merge*.

*im*merge

26. Generalizing again, suppose there were a prefix *hub-*. If it were combined with the root *rain*, which of the following combinations would it make?
    hubrain   hurain
    hurrain   hubbain

hurrain

27. When you see *suf-*, *sug-*, *sum-*, *suc-*, *sup-*, *sur-*, and *sus-*, remember that you may be seeing a variant or assimilated form of the prefix ___.

sub-

When you learn to apply one prefix that unlocks the meanings of over a thousand common English words you have, in a sense, stepped up your vocabulary-building efforts to supersonic speed. Lean on your knowledge of *sub-* in taking the following difficult test.

1. If you're told to get a *subaltern,* you should start looking for   (1) a calibrated barometer; (2) a handwriting expert; (3) a part for a gasoline engine; or (4) someone of inferior rank.

2. *Subliminal* means   (1) below the threshold of consciousness; (2) a projecting appendage; (3) limitless; (4) terminal.

3. *Submontane* means   (1) monetary; (2) monastic; (3) beneath a mountain; (4) a ravine.

4. *Subsume* means to   (1) dig out; (2) spend lavishly; (3) put under the proper heading; (4) begin all over again.

5. *Succinct* means   (1) exact; (2) concise; (3) tight; (4) juicy.

1. _____

2. _____

3. _____

4. _____

5. _____

A *subaltern* is "under" someone else in rank. As you might expect, the root *altern* comes from the Latin word *alter,* meaning "other," as in our words *alter ego, alternate, alter,* and *altercation. Subliminal* is a technical word from psychology which describes sensations not consciously perceived, hence under the level of conscious awareness. *Submontane* is, of course, "under" a mountain. And when you classify information under a heading, you *subsume* it—from *sub* + *sumere* (to take), as in our words *assume, consume,* or *resume.* If something is *succinct,* it is said with an "under" supply of words, not an oversupply, hence, *concise* or *brief.*

19

IN

1. *In-* and *in-*, the identical twins of the prefix world, are found in over 2,000 English words of a desk-sized dictionary. One *in-* means "not," the other "in" or "into." In which of the following words do you have *in-* meaning "in" or "into"?

   infirm
   inside
   inactive

   inside

2. In which of the following words do you have *in-* meaning "not"?

   intrude
   investigate
   invisible

   invisible

3. You have only three variants to note, *ir- il-*, and *im-*. If *to assimilate* is "to make similar," you would expect *in-* plus *lustrate* to give __*lustrate*.

   *il*lustrate

131

*ir*regular

4. Before *regular* you would expect *in-* to become __*regular* or not regular.

n

5. Which one of the following letters does *not* require bringing the lips together in its pronunciation—*p*, *m, n,* or *b*?

*im*bibe

6. Before the labials *p, m,* and *b* the prefix *in-* becomes *im-,* as in __*bibe.*

lips

7. If you are alert, you build a vocabulary just from reading. From the last two items, for example, you would infer that labials are letters articulated mainly by the ____.

*in*land

8. In words of English origin, such as *land, in-* is usually unchanged, giving us the form __*land.*

*en*close

9. *In-* has a French form *en-.* If you close something "into" a letter you either inclose or __close it.

*em*brace

10. Just as *in-* plus *bue* equals *imbue,* so *en-* plus *brace* would give __*brace.*

emerge

11. Remember the meaning check. For example, which of the following words does *not* have the meaning "in" or "into"?

encircle   embrace
enclose   emerge

enfeeble

12. Sometimes the meaning "to make or cause to be" is uppermost. In which word is this meaning dominant?

enfeeble
enthrone

13. One may migrate into or out of a country. The prefix makes the difference. Add *in-* to *migrate* and you get the word meaning "to migrate into," "_____."

immigrate

14. Add an assimilated form of *ex-*, meaning "out," to *migrate* and you get _*migrate*, meaning "to migrate out."

*e*migrate

15. If explosion is a bursting "out," an implosion would be a bursting __.

in

16. If you have an automobile tire you can either de-flate or __flate it.

*in*flate

17. The Latin word *lumen* means "light." Light coming "into" a room will i_____ate it.

*illumi*nate

18. The Latin verb *rigare* means "to water." When water is channeled "into" fields to supply moisture for crops, we call it _____ing.

*irrigat*ing

19. The first line of a paragraph is usually set in from the margin or __dented.

*in*dented

20. The Latin noun *pes, pedis,* means "foot." When your foot gets entangled "in" something so as to hinder your progress, we say it __pedes progress.

*im*pedes

21. Then when you get your foot "out," your progress is __pedited.

*ex*pedited

rushes into
things

22. Use prefix meaning in defining an impetuous person as one who
    enjoys things
    rushes into things
    damages things.

*im*plicate

23. The new evidence uncovered by detectives tended to __plicate another.

import

24. The opposite of *export* is _____.

*in*augurated

25. When the president is formally inducted "into" office, the president is __augurated.

in*cision*

26. When a surgeon operates, the surgeon usually makes an in_____.

impress

27. To inculcate something on your mind is to
    impress it   read it
    calculate it   forget it.

increment

28. When you invest some money you can take resulting loss, or decrement, or the opposite—a gain, or _____.

not, in or into

29. To recapitulate, the prefixes *in-* and *in-* mean "___" and "__" or "____."

in-

30. The variant forms *ir-*, *il-*, and *im-* may be forms of the prefix __.

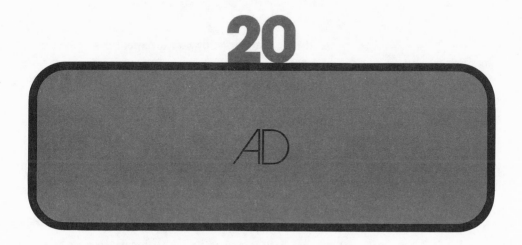

20

AD

1. The common meaning of *ad-* is "to" or "toward."
   If *imply* means "fold in," and *reply*, " fold back,"
   the word which literally would mean "fold to" is
   ap___.   ap*ply*

2. *Ad-* is the most changeable prefix in the English
   language. Remember that *assimilate* means "to
   make similar." When you add *ad-* to a root begin-   ap-
   ning with *p* you get __, as in __ply.   ap*ply*

3. Try pronouncing *adclaim* rapidly and you will
   soon be reminded that before a *c*, *ad-* becomes __.   ac-

4. If *ad-* becomes *ac-* before a *c*, you would expect *ad-*   ag-
   to become __ before a *g*, as in __*gravate*.   ag*gravate*

135

*af*fliction

5. Before a root beginning with *f*, you would expect an assimilative change in *ad-*, as in __*fliction.*

*al*luring

6. If she has a smile that lures men to her, there is reason to call her __luring.

an-
*an*notation

7. And before an *n,* you would expect *ad-* to become __, as in __*notation.*

ar-
*ar*rest

8. Before an *r,* the assimilated form of *ad-,* __, would appear, as in __*rest.*

*as*similate

9. The word which both names and illustrates the variant changes you are now studying is the word __*similate.*

*at*tract

10. Before a root beginning with a certain consonant, the *d* in *ad-* is assimilated, or made like that consonant; for example, *ad-* plus *tract* makes __*tract.*

*a*scend

11. One other type of assimilative change occurs before a root beginning with *sc, sp,* or *st*—the final *d* is dropped—as when adding *ad-* to *scend* to make _*scend.*

apology

12. With ten variant forms, *ad-* is not always easy to spot. With all but the last variant, however, the sign of the double consonant will help you determine which words contain a form of *ad-*. Which of the following does not contain *ad-?*

    attempt   appease
    arrive   apology

double

13. Such words as *affinity, aggrieve, alliance,* and *annex* all contain evidence, the sign of the _____ consonant, for suspecting the presence of *ad-*.

14. Another rule-of-thumb check is the prefix-substitution check. In which word can you substitute another prefix?

    apply
    apple

    apply (to make *reply, comply,* or *supply*)

15. The meaning check is still another to remember. In which of the following words is the meaning "to" or "toward" strongest?

    advance
    adrift

    advance

16. With the *a-* form of *ad-*, watch for possible confusion with the Greek prefix *a-*, meaning "not," which is different from *ad-*, meaning "__" or "toward."

    to

17. For example, which of the following words contains the Greek prefix *a-* (meaning "not")?

    atypical
    aspect

    atypical

18. With the prefix meaning of *ad-* in mind, you would infer that the strange word *adit* probably means

    an approach or entrance
    a farewell or parting
    a number.

    an approach or entrance

19. Judging from the prefix, the strange word *adnate* probably means

    lowered   separated
    hindered   joined.

    joined

20. From the prefix meaning "to" and the root *nectere*, "to tie or bind," comes our word describing an addition to a building—an __*nex*.

    annex

*af*fluent

21. When riches flow in great abundance "to" some-one, he is rightly called wealthy or __fluent.

*ad*vocating

22. When you support something, calling others to accept your point of view, you are __vocating its support.

*ag*gressive

23. If a regressive move is a move "back," an _____- ____ move would mean a move "to" or "toward."

*ac*cept

24. Remember, you can either reject or __cept an idea.

*af*fixes

25. If a prefix is added "before" the root and a suffix "after," both are added "to" the root and are there-fore __fixes.

*as*semble

26. When you bring people to a certain spot, you may be said to __semble them there.

*as*sign

27. When you lay out a lesson or indicate a task, you are said to __sign it.

ad-

28. Whenever you see *ap-, ac-, ag-, af-, al-, an-, ar-, as-, at-,* or just plan *a-,* remember it may be a form of the prefix __, the most changeable prefix in the English language.

Opposites Review Test

Now that you have completed your study of the twenty most im-portant prefixes, you should work with some of the test words com-monly found in such exams as the Scholastic Aptitude Tests, civil service tests, scholarship tests, and the like. For example:

	Prefix	**Meaning**	**Opposite meaning**	**Opposite word**
eclectic	*ex-*	out	in	(1) extravert;
				(2) all-inclusive;
				(3) lengthy;
				(4) conferring;
				(5) strengthen

If you know the word, fine. If you don't, look for a prefix you know—in this case the prefix *ex-*, meaning "out." The opposite of "out" is "in." Look for a choice that is the opposite of "out." If you are not choosing, you are not picking something "out" but leaving it "in," suggesting that 2 is the right answer. In the following, look for opposite meanings to italic words.

1. *Discrete:*   (1) wise; (2) judicious; (3) joined; (4) shortened

1. _____

2. *Extrinsic:*   (1) additional; (2) common; (3) uncultivated; (4) internal

2. _____

3. *Consensus:*   (1) poll; (2) disharmony; (3) conference; (4) opinion

3. _____

4. *Indigenous:*   (1) foreign; (2) destitute; (3) insulting; (4) common

4. _____

5. *Desuetude:*   (1) spasmodic action; (2) fatigue; (3) state of use; (4) helpfulness

5. _____

6. *Absolve:*   (1) thank; (2) blame; (3) discover; (4) repent

6. _____

7. *Intransigent:*   (1) impossible; (2) reconcilable; (3) high-flying; (4) sharp

7. _____

8. *Ingenuous:*   (1) speedy; (2) troublesome; (3) talented; (4) plotting

8. _____

9. *Disinterested:* (1) opposed; (2) contemptuous; (3) careless; (4) biased

9. _____

10. *Propitiate:* (1) anger; (2) approach; (3) agree; (4) praise

10. _____

11. *Ineluctable:* (1) avoidable; (2) inscrutable; (3) chosen; (4) arranged

11. _____

12. *Retral:* (1) back; (2) trained; (3) forward; (4) quiet

12. _____

13. *Ebullient:* (1) bubbling; (2) bizarre; (3) dull; (4) bulky

13. _____

14. *Enclave:* (1) separate country; (2) settlement; (3) prison; (4) papal edict

14. _____

15. *Dissonance:* (1) disapproval; (2) disaster; (3) harmony; (4) disparity

15. _____

16. *Effrontery:* (1) bad taste; (2) conceit; (3) shyness; (4) commonness

16. _____

17. *Reticent:* (1) truthful; (2) talkative; (3) quiet; (4) tired

17. _____

18. *Assiduous:* (1) courteous; (2) slow; (3) methodical; (4) careless

18. _____

19. *Extirpate:* (1) smear; (2) clean; (3) renew; (4) encourage

19. _____

20. *Obviate:* (1) seize; (2) reform; (3) simplify; (4) make necessary

20. _____

(Answers on page 257.)

Difficult, wasn't it? But think how much more difficult for anyone who didn't know the opposites test form or wasn't aware of prefix meanings.

Review Test IV

A. In the blank after each prefix in the left-hand column, write the number, from the right-hand list, of the common meaning of the prefix. The same meaning may apply to more than one prefix. Some meanings will not be used at all.

1. *in-*	_____	1. away
		2. not
2. *com-*	_____	3. near
		4. together, with
3. *sub-*	_____	5. under
		6. into
4. *in-*	_____	7. to, towards
		8. up
5. *ad-*	_____	

B. In each of the following sets of words, there is one word that does *not* contain the prefix found in the rest of the words in that set. Using the principles in Unit 2, find that word and enter the appropriate number in the blank at the right.

1. (1) indigo; (2) import; (3) irradiate; (4) illustrate   1. _____

2. (1) collaborate; (2) comic; (3) correspond; (4) cooperate; (5) converge   2. _____

3. (1) succinct; (2) sustain; (3) support; (4) suffuse; (5) submerge; (6) sully   3. _____

4. (1) incurable; (2) infallible; (3) ideal; (4) illiterate; (5) irrational   4. _____

5. (1) approach; (2) accord; (3) aggressive; (4) after; (5) attract; (6) assist; (7) arrange; (8) allocate   5. _____

Use your knowledge of prefixes to fill in the blanks below.

1. If *regress* is to "step back," an entrance or place to "step in" would be an ___gress.

2. If *ingress* is a place to "step in or into," a place to "step out" would be an exit or ___gress.

3. If an *egress* is a place to "step out," when you "step toward" someone as if to fight, you are acting ___gressively.

4. If *aggressive* means "stepping to or toward," when a formal assembly comes to "step together," it is rightly called a ___gress.

5. If you now forget that *gress* means to "step," you will be taking a "step back" or ___gressing, instead of ___gressing.

(*Answers on page 257.*)

Prefix Mini-Review

To complete this section on prefixes, here's a mini-review of all twenty prefixes—the most important shortcuts in the English language. They're so important you should know them all perfectly. And here's the review to insure that kind of mastery. Use this review from time to time as needed to keep your mind refreshed.

Remember, you have three review patterns.

1. This is the easiest. Cover the right-hand column with your three-by-five-inch card. See if you can supply the common meaning or meanings for each prefix. Move the card down for an immediate check when you have an answer.

2. For a more difficult check, cover both right-hand columns. See if you can supply both the suggested mnemonic and the common meaning.

3. For the most difficult review, cover both left-hand columns. See if you can supply both mnemonic and prefix to fit each meaning. Again, check your answers immediately.

Prefix	Suggested Mnemonic	Common Meaning
1. *pre-*	preview	before
2. *de-*	depress, depart, defrost	down, away, reverse
3. *mono-*	monopoly	one

4. *inter-*	intermission, interspersed	between, among
5. *un-*	untidy	not
6. *re-*	refund, reread	back, again
7. *trans-*	transport, transcend	across, beyond
8. *pro-*	progress, prolabor	forward, for
9. *non-*	nonresident	not
10. *epi-*	epidemic, epidermis	upon, above
11. *mis-*	misspell	wrong, wrongly
12. *ob-*	obstinant, objective	against, to
13. *ex-*	exit	out
14. *dis-*	dissect, dispatch	apart, away
15. *in-*	insecure	not
16. *com-*	companion, connect	with, together
17. *sub-*	submerge	under
18. *in-*	inflate	in, into
19. *ad-*	advance	to, toward
20. *over-*	overpass, overseer, overflow, overeat	above, beyond, lower, excessive

Optional Review Essay

As a further means of sharpening awareness of contextual clues and as a review of all prefixes studied so far, fill in the blanks with the appropriate prefixes. The common meaning of the prefix is given in the margin. You are not asked to identify *all* prefixes. When words with prefixes are repeated, they are not always structured with blanks to be filled.

Notice as you work through this selection how prefix knowledge helps you both understand and remember words more readily. For example, induction is by derivation a leading "into" a generalization. Given certain facts, you use them to lead you "into" a generalization. When you move "away" from a general law to an individual case or situation, you are said to deduce certain things about it.

Suppose you notice that a prelude is something played before a service and that a postlude is something played after. With those two instances in mind, when you reason that *lude* probably means "play," what process did you use to arrive at that conclusion—induction or deduction? Obviously most of the frames in this text encourage you to use methods of reasoning and scientific investigation in learning and using words and word parts.

In case you wish to move right ahead with your study of the four-teen words, you'll find two much shorter review passages on pages 242 and 243 to use for prefix review.

All Men Are Scientists*

Thomas Henry Huxley

into
under
into
into/into
away
forward
together, with

into

through
back, again/away

out

before/out
apart, not

together, with/
through/apart, not/
together, with
apart, not
together, with
not
to, toward

out, beyond/
back, again
in
away

Scientific ___vestigation is not, as many people seem to ___pose, some kind of modern black art. You might easily gather this ___pression from the manner in which many per-sons speak of scientific ___quiry, or talk about ___ductive and ___ductive philosophy, or the principles of the "Baconian philosphy." I do ___test that, of the vast number of cants in this world, there are none, to my mind, so ___temptible as the pseudo-scientific cant which is talked about the "Baconian philosophy."

To hear people talk about the great Chancellor—and a very great man he certainly was, —you would think that it was he who had ___vented science, and that there was no such thing as sound reasoning before the time of Queen Elizabeth! Of course you say, that cannot possibly be true; you ___ceive, on a moment's ___flection, that such an idea is ___surdly wrong. . . .

The method of scientific investigation is nothing but the ___pression of the necessary mode of working of the hu-man mind. It is simply the mode at which all phenomena are reasoned about, rendered ___cise and ___act. There is no more ___ference, but there is just the same kind of difference, be-tween the mental operations of a man of science and those of an ordinary person, as there is between the operations and methods of a baker or of a butcher weighing out his goods in ___mon scales, and the operations of a chemist in ___forming a ___ficult and ___plex analysis by means of his balance and finely-graduated weights. It is not that the action of the scales in the one case, and the balance in the other, ___fer in the principles of their ___struction or manner of working; but the beam of one is set on an ___finitely finer axis than the other, and of course turns by the ___dition of a much smaller weight.

You will understand this better, perhaps, if I give you some familiar ___ample. You have all heard it ___peated, I dare say, that men of science work by means of ___duction and ___duction, and that by the help of these operations, they, in a

*From *Darwiniana,* 1893.

sort of sense, wring from Nature certain other things, which
are called natural laws, and causes, and that out of these, by
some cunning skill of their own, they build up hypotheses and
theories. And it is imagined by many, that the operations of
the ___mon mind can be by no means ___pared with these   together, with/
___cesses, and that they have to be ___cquired by a sort of   together, with
special ___nticeship to the craft. To hear all these large   for/to
words, you would think that the mind of a man of science   to/before
must be ___stituted ___ferently from that of his fellow men;   together/apart
but if you will not be frightened by terms, you will ___cover   apart
that you are quite wrong, and that all these terrible ___paratus   to
are being used by yourselves every day and every hour of
your lives.

    There is a well-known ___cident in one of Molière's   into
plays, where the author makes the hero ___press ___bounded   out/not
delight on being told that he had been talking prose during
the whole of his life. In the same way, I trust, that you will
take ___fort, and be ___lighted with yourselves, on the dis-   with/down
covery that you have been acting on the principles of ___duc-   in
tive and ___ductive philosophy during the same period. Prob-   down
ably there is not one who has not in the course of the day had
___casion to set in motion a ___plex train of reasoning, of the   against/with
very same kind, though ___fering of course in degree, as that   apart
which a scientific man goes through in tracing the causes of
natural phenomena.

    A very trivial circumstance will serve to ___emplify this.   out
Suppose you go into a fruiterer's shop, wanting an apple,—
you take up one, and, on biting it, you find it is sour; you look
at it, and see that it is hard and green. You take up another
one, and that too is hard, green, and sour. The shopman offers
you a third; but, before biting it, you ___amine it, and find that   out
it is hard and green, and you ___mediately say that you will not   into
have it, as it must be sour, like those that you have already
tried.

    Nothing can be more simple than that, you think; but if
you will take the trouble to analyse and trace out into its
logical elements what has been done by the mind, you will be
greatly surprised. In the first place, you have ___formed the   through
operation of ___duction. You found that, in two ___periences,   in/out
hardness and greenness in apples went together with sour-
ness. It was so in the first case, and it was ___firmed by the   together
second. True, it is a very small basis, but still it is enough to
make an induction from; you generalize the facts, and you
___pect to find sourness in apples where you get hardness and   out
greenness. You found upon that a general law, that all hard
and green apples are sour; and that, so far as it goes, is a
___fect induction. Well, having got your natural law in this   through

against

before
before/together, with
out
forward/down

under

apart

back, again

out
against

against

out/to
apart/under
not/to/
together
through
out
out/back
to/together
toward
against

out/before
down, away

out/under
into/to, towards
with
out/forward/away

way, when you are ___fered another apple which you find is hard and green, you say, "All hard and green apples are sour; this apple is hard and green, therefore this apple is sour." That train of reasoning is what logicians call a syllogism, and has all its various parts and terms—its major ___mise, its minor ___mise, and its ___clusion. And, by the help of further reasoning, which, if drawn out, would have to be ___hibited in two or three other syllogisms, you ___rive at your final ___termination, "I will not have that apple." So that, you see, you have, in the first place, established a law by induction, and upon that you have founded a deduction, and reasoned out the special conclusion of the particular case. Well now, ___pose, having got your law, that at some time afterwards, you are ___cussing the qualities of apples with a friend: you will say to him, "It is a very curious thing,—but I find that all hard and green apples are sour!" Your friend says to you, "But how do you know that?" You at once ___ply, "Oh, because I have tried them over and over again, and have always found them to be so." Well, if we were talking science instead of common sense, we should call that an ___perimental verification. And, if still ___posed, you go further, and say, "I have heard from the people of Somersetshire and Devonshire, where a large number of apples are grown, that they have ___served the same thing. It is also found to be the case in Normandy, and in North America. In short, I find it to be the universal ___perience of mankind wherever ___tention has been ___rected to the ___ject." Whereupon, your friend, unless he is a very ___reasonable man, ___grees with you, and is ___vinced that you are quite right in the ___clusion you have drawn. He believes, although ___haps he does not know he believes it, that the more ___tensive verifications are,—that the more frequently ___periments have been made, and ___sults of the same kind ___rived, at,—that the more varied the ___ditions under which the same results are___tained, the more certain is the ultimate conclusion, and he ___putes the question no further. He sees that the experiment has been tried under all sorts of conditions, as to time, place, and people, with the same result; and he says with you, therefore, that the law you have laid down must be a good one, and he must believe it.

In science we do the same thing;—the philosopher ___ercises ___cisely the same faculties, though in a much more ___licate manner. In scientific inquiry it becomes a matter of duty to ___pose a ___posed law to every possible kind of verification, and to take care, moreover, that this is done ___tentionally, and not left to a mere ___cident, as in the case of the apples. And in science, as in common life, our ___fidence in a law is in ___act ___portion to the ___sence of varia-

tion in the result of our experimental verifications. For
____stance, if you let go your grasp of an article you may have
in your hand, it will ____mediately fall to the ground. That is a
very ____mon verification of one of the best established laws of
nature — that of gravitation. The method by which men of
science establish the ____istence of that law is ____actly the same
as that by which we have established the trivial ____position
about the sourness of hard and green apples. But we believe it
in such an ____tensive, thorough, and ____hesitating manner
because the universal ____perience of mankind verifies it, and
we can verify it ourselves at any time; and that is the strongest
possible foundation on which any natural law can rest. . . .

in
into
together, with

out/out
forward

out/not/
out

(To emphasize the commonness of the twenty prefixes you've studied,
over three hundred students were asked to check the first twenty words
in a current newspaper article. In ninety-nine per cent of the checks,
students found at least one of the twenty prefixes — excellent scientific
verification of their key importance. Try it yourself with a newspaper or
magazine — just twenty words.

PART THREE

ROOTS

21

CAPERE

1. In English as in Latin, verbs have a variety of forms.
   We say, "I run," "You run," "He run_."

   runs

2. Fill in the corect form of the verb *run* in the following sentence. "I was _____ down the street."

   running

3. Some forms are made by adding letters, as in *runs*
   and *running*. Others involve internal change, as in
   the sentence, "Yesterday we r_n home."

   ran

4. The infinitive form is made in still another way, by
   adding a *to* before the verb, giving us the form "__
   run."

   to

5. The infinitive form, with the *to* either understood or expressed, is the form we use in talking about a verb. We therefore speak of the verb *run* (*to* is understood) or the verb __ *run*.

to

6. With Latin verbs, most infinitive forms end in -*ere*, -*are*, or -*ire*. If the Latin verb *capio* means "I take," the form *capere* probably means "__ take."

to

7. To help spot English words derived from Latin verbs, drop the infinitive ending to get the base form. For example, the base form of *capere* would be ___.

cap

8. Since our word *capture* contains *cap*, you have reason to suspect it is derived from the Latin verb _____, meaning "to take or seize."

capere

9. Go a step farther, however. Always check form with meaning. Does the word *capture* contain the idea of "taking" or "seizing"? ___

yes

10. *Capture* appears related to *capere*, "to take or seize," in both form and _____.

meaning
(or idea)

11. Finally, a glance at the dictionary will corroborate the fact that *capture* is derived from the Latin verb _____.

capere

12. Thinking in terms of these rule-of-thumb checks, which of the following two words is derived from *capere*?
captivity
capstone

captivity

13. Now put this useful shortcut to use. A small, soluble, gelatin container designed to "take" or enclose a dose of medicine is called a _ _ _ sule.

*cap*sule

14. If you have real ability to "take" charge, we can speak of you as competent or _ _ _ _ _ _ _, literally, "able to take."

capable

15. If someone spoke of a capacious container, you would assume it would _ _ _ _ a lot to fill it.

take

16. Because it "takes" your attention, the heading, title, or subtitle, as of a picture, is called a _ _ _ tion.

caption

17. As with English verbs, be alert to discover variant forms. For example, when you accept something, you _ _ _ _ it from the donor.

take

18. The *cept* in *accept* is very similar to the *capt* in *capture,* the kind of change we see in *run* and *ran.* Furthermore, *accept* and *capture* both obviously contain the idea of _ _ _ _ _ _ _ or seizing.

taking

19. A glance at *accept* in the dictionary lets you know that it is actually derived from the Latin verb _ _ _ _ _ _ _, "to take or seize."

capere

20. Alert yourself to variations in English words. When you practice a deception on someone, you are said to de_ _ _ _ _ _ him.

deceive

21. Use the chain reaction of analogy to extend understanding. *Deceive* is to *deception* as *receive* is to _ _ _ _ _ _ _ _ _.

reception

deceitful

22. What related form of *deceive* and *deception* means "tending to deceive"? _____ful

recipient

23. When you receive an award, you are a re___ient of it or the one who "takes" it.

receipt

24. If you are the recipient of money, you may be asked to give a written acknowledgment that you "took" it, something for the donor to "take" as proof of delivery. This is called a re_____.

captivating

25. Always look for the idea of "taking." If someone "takes" your attention because of her beauty and charm, you have reason to call her ___tivating.

exception

26. If you find a case that does not follow the general rule, you call it an ex_____ion because you have to "take" it out of the general category and deal with it separately.

principal

27. In a school, the one who "takes" top place in authority is called the school prin_____.

participant

28. When you take part in some activity, you are a parti___ant.

cap

29. Although *cept, cip, ceiv, ceipt,* and *ceit* are possible variant forms of *capere,* the most common form of all is the ___ form.

Capere Review Exercise

To heighten your awareness of how frequently you meet and use words derived from *capere,* fill in the blanks in the following context with the appropriate words derived from *capere.* The listing at the bottom of the page will suggest some possibilities

With this book, you're developing to the full your (1) ~~precepts~~ *capacity* to identify and use those word parts of (2) *principal* importance. (3) *Emancipate* yourself from old ways of dealing with words. Apply the new (4) *precepts* introduced here. (5) *Perceive* words in a different light. (6) *Accept* the fact that you are (7) *capable* of (8) *anticipating* how the dictionary defines a word. To be sure, there are (9) *excep-tions*. But if you (10) *occupy* yourself with the study of word parts, you'll soon see real improvement.

except, accept, occupy, capable, perceive, precepts, capacity, incipient, municipal, capacious, principal, captivity, emancipate, exceptions, susceptible, participate, anticipating

(The words are arranged in order of length, from shortest to longest. If necessary, use the number of letters to help you select the right word from the list.)

(Answers on page 257.)

22

PONERE

1. *Ponere,* "to put or place," makes an important contribution to English. Dropping the infinitive *-ere* gives you the form most commonly found in English, the base form ___.

pon

2. If an article is made by "putting" several parts together, you can speak of them as com___ent parts.

com*pon*ent

3. The number 3 in x^3 is a figure that is "put" above and out to the right and is, therefore, called an ex_____.

ex*pon*ent

4. Someone pitted against you in a contest or game is your op_____.

op*pon*ent

5. When *pon* comes at the end of a word, with no suffix following, you usually add a final *e,* as in the word meaning "to defer" or "*put* off until later" — the word *post_____.*

*post*pone

6. Now let your knowledge of English lead you to another form of *ponere.* An opponent is not on the same side as you but on the op_____e side.

op*posite*

7. Sometimes, as with *opposite,* there is an *e* added. At other times you have no *e.* For example, when you go to the bank to "put" some money into your account, you de_____ it.

de*posit*

8. If you want employment — a "place" for yourself — try to find a _____ion with the government.

*posit*ion

9. When you "put" words together, as when writing themes in school, you call the result a com_____-____.

com*position*

10. If you know the two-letter prefix meaning "out," you should be able to build the word meaning to "put out" information, explain, or make clear. "I wrote a brilliant _____ion on relativity."

*exposit*ion

11. Remember what happens to *in-* when it is followed by *p?* If you do, you will know that when one person is "put" "in" another person's way without right or invitation, it is an _____.

imposition

12. Think of the prefix meaning "before." Look at the phrases "in the road" and "by me." Since such words as *in* and *by* are usually "put before" a noun or pronoun, they are called _____.

prepositions

trans*position*

13. When you transform 592 to 529, you have made a trans_____ of the 9 and the 2.

*posit*ive

14. You can be indefinite about some things, but sure, or ____tive, about others.

put
place

15. By now whenever you see a *pon, pone, posit,* or *posite* you should think of *ponere,* meaning "to ___ or _____."

trans*posed*

16. Do not stop here, though. Let us see if you can discover still another variant. When there is a transposition of two numbers, we can say they have been trans_____.

pose

17. As with *pon,* which sometimes is *pone,* so it is with *pos,* which is sometimes ____.

pos

18. Yes, when you drop the *it* from *posit,* you get the variant form ___.

proposal

19. When a man makes an offer of marriage, we say he made a _____ of marriage.

posts

20. For another variant, suppose we turn to farmers. When they "put" up a fence, they begin by putting _____ at certain intervals along a line.

im*postor*

21. Yes, *post* is another common variant. It is found in a word meaning a fraud who deceives by pretending to be someone else, or an im_____.

postage

22. And remember, when you "put" or "place" a stamp on a letter, that stamp is called a _____ stamp.

23. (Be careful not to confuse *post-*, the prefix meaning "behind" or "after," and *post*, a variant form of the Latin verb _____.)

ponere

24. When a person stands erectly we say he has good ____ure.

*post*ure

25. When you "put" leaves, vegetable refuse, and the like "together" for subsequent fertilization of the soil, you call it a com____ pile.

com*post*

26. In chemistry when you "put" two or more elements "together" (combine them), you have a *compound*. You would infer from meaning that *pound* is probably a variant of the Latin verb _____.

ponere

27. When you "put" forth some pet notions or ideas of yours on a subject, you are said to pro_____ them.

pro*pound*

28. By now you can begin to see how many of our English words are derived from *ponere*, meaning to ___ or _____.

put
place

29. Now you should be better able to deal with such difficult words as *juxtaposition*, which means

side by side
moving along slowly
falling rapidly.

side by side

30. When you spot a form of *ponere* in the word *juxtaposition*, you are ready to say it means "to put or place *juxta*, or ____ by ____."

side by *side*

31. The two most common three-letter combinations from *ponere* are ___ and ___, with *pound* and *post* also to be noted.

pon and *pos*

Ponere Review Exercise

Fill in the numbered blanks in the following brief context with words derived from *ponere*. If needed, look at the extended listing at the bottom of the page for help.

Capitalize on the power of (1) _____ thinking as you work on vocabulary. That puts you in an ideal (2) _____. When you (3) _____ a letter, don't (4) _____ use of the words you're studying. Using new words is so satisfying it even helps your (5) _____. And when you finish your letter and put on the right (6) _____, (7) _____ it in the nearest mail (8) _____, on the (9) _____ that it will be carried by the next (10) ____ to its proper destination.

post, impost, expose, deposit, postage, posture, compose, propound, opposite, postpone, positive, impostor, position, component, exposition, depository, disposition, supposition, transposition

(*Answers on page 257.*)

23

TENERE

1. The Latin verb *tenere* means "to have or hold." *Tenio* is the first person singular, present tense, and means "I ____ or ____."

have
hold

2. The *-ere* in *tenere* indicates the infinitive form. To get the form most frequently seen in English, drop the three-letter infinitive ending, leaving ___.

ten

3. The third person singular, present tense, of *tenere* is found by dropping the infinitive ending and adding the ending *-et*, giving us the word _____.

tenet

4. *Tenet* — the Latin word meaning "he or she holds" — comes over into English without change to mean "a principle or doctrine ____ by someone or some group."

held

*tena*ciously

5. Now for some English derivatives. When you "hold" on firmly and stubbornly, you hold on ___aciously.

*ten*acity

6. If you won't let go easily, we say you "hold" on with bulldog ___acity.

lieu*tenant*

7. The officer who "holds" the authority in lieu of the captain is called a lieu _____.

tenant

8. One who, as a renter, "holds" a room, apartment, or house, is spoken of as a _____.

*ten*ement

9. An apartment building, since it is intended to "hold" a number of different families may be spoken of as a ___ement house.

*ten*ure

10. When teachers have worked in a school system for a set period of time, their "hold" on the position is considered permanent and they are said to have ___ure.

*ten*able

11. In military language, a position that can be "held" is called a ___able position.

de*ten*tion

12. To discover variant forms, take English words that you already know, such as the word *de___tion.*

de*tain*

13. You would not say, "Don't let me detention you any longer." You would say, "Don't let me de_____ you."

tenere

14. This shows that you recognize *tain* as another form of the Latin verb _____.

15. This opens the way to a whole new family of words. *Detention* is to *detain* as *retention* is to _____.

retain

16. If a drinking glass "holds" some milk, we say it _____ milk.

contains

17. If the facts are relevant, they can be said to per____ to the matter in question.

per*tain*

18. A floor, supported or "held" from below, is usually sus_____, or held up, by joists.

sus*tained*

19. It is with food that we all main____ life.

main*tain*

20. When you hold out hospitality to someone, inviting him to your house, you are said to enter____ him.

enter*tain*

21. If *ab-* or *abs-* means "away," when you "hold" yourself "away" from smoking you are said to _____.

abstain

22. If you abstain completely, this is spoken of, not as total *abstainence,* but as total *abs___ence.*

abs*tin*ence

23. In this way your knowledge of English brings you to *tin* as still another variant from the Latin verb _____.

tenere

24. If you read of someone's pertinacity, you would expect that person to ____ on with persistence.

hold

25. When something "holds" the same pattern over a period of time, we say it has con___ued in that way for that time.

con*tin*ued

continent

26. A large and extensive land mass (something "held" together) is often spoken of as a con_____.

holding

27. Now whenever you see a *ten, tent, tain, tin,* or *tinu* in a word, look for the idea of having or _____.

have

hold

28. A word of caution. Beware of possible confusion between *tendere,* "to stretch," and *tenere,* "to _____ or _____."

tenere

29. The forms *ten, tain,* and *tin* are all common forms from the Latin verb _____.

<u>Tenere</u> Review Exercise

Fill in the numbered blanks in the following brief context with words derived from *tenere.* Use the list below for help.

Don't be (1) _____ until you've explored (2) _____ the various forms (3) _____ to <u>tenere</u>. Reviews of this kind help you (4) _____ what you've learned as well as (5) _____ new insights. As you (6) _____ your study, (7) _____ high interest by using any new words in your writing or speaking. That's a sure way to (8) _____ good vocabulary growth. That provides (9) _____ spaced review, so important for best results. I hope you'll find it (10) _____ as well.

obtain, retain, tenure, tenant, content, sustain, abstain, maintain, continue, tenement, continual, tenacious, appertain, pertaining, abstinence, tenaciously, incontinent, entertaining, countenances.

(Answers on page 257.)

24

DUCERE

1. The Latin verb *ducere,* "to lead," comes over into English without the *-ere* sign of the infinitive, giving us the base form ___ to watch for.

   duc

2. If a certain setting "leads" to or contributes to a feeling of restfulness, we can say it is con___ive to rest.

   con*duc*ive

3. To reinforce root meanings, always try to use them when dealing with derivatives. For example, with *conducive,* from *ducere* ("to lead"), think of a situation conducive to learning as one _____ you in that direction.

   leading

4. Some think *education* is a pouring in of information, but the word itself means literally "to ____ out."

   lead

165

reduce

5. A silent *e* after *duc* is common. For example, when someone goes on a special diet to lure away excess poundage, we say he is trying to re_____.

produces

6. If a company manufactures cars, it literally "leads them forward," or pro_____ them.

reproduce

7. When you produce a picture one or more times, as in printing, you are said to re_____it.

leader

8. Your root knowledge should let you infer that the Italians called Mussolini *Il Duce* because he was their _____.

introduction

9. Now call on your knowledge of English to lead you to a common variant. When you introduce someone, you make an intro_____.

seduces

10. If a man encourages or "leads" a girl to give up her virginity, we say he se_____ her. And if anything is tempting or strongly attractive we can speak of it as seductive.

duke

11. Some are by title "leaders" in their country. To get the title, change the *c* in *duce* to *k* to make _____.

duchess

12. Still another variant is introduced when a duke marries; his wife then becomes a _____ess.

conduit

13. For still another variant, think of how electric wires are "led" through walls. For that purpose a metal tube, either rigid or flexible, called a con-_____, is used.

14. Now that you know the variant forms *duc, duct, duk, duch,* and *duit,* let's take a closer look. One who "leads" a group on a tour is called a tour con-_____.

con*ductor*

15. Something that is produced is known as a pro____.

pro*duct*

16. If your vocabulary development is facilitated by studying roots of words, we can call this a pro____-ive method.

pro*ductive*

17. A copper wire is able to carry, or _____, electricity.

conduct

18. If an aquatic plant is a water plant, you would call a conduit for bringing water from a distant source an aque____.

aque*duct*

19. If *viatic* means "of a road," the word describing a structure to carry a road over a valley or gorge would be a _____.

viaduct

20. A pliant, easily bent metal strip is ____ile in nature.

*duct*ile

21. With root meaning in mind, if a detective educed important information from a suspect, he would probably

lose it   pass it by
draw it out   discover it.

draw it out

22. To reason from the known down to the unknown is called de____ive reasoning.

de*duct*ive

inductive

23. The opposite, reasoning from the particular to the general, is called in_____ reasoning.

to bring in
reasons

24. Using root knowledge, you would expect *adduce* to mean

to remain still
to bring in reasons
to be confused.

to take away
character

25. And you would surmise that *to traduce* would be

to take away character
to fear discovery
to disagree with.

26. Although *duit, duke, duct, duch,* and *duce* are all possible derivatives of *ducere,* the most common form is ____.

duc

Ducere Review Exercise

Fill in the numbered blanks in the following brief context with words derived from *ducere.* Use the listing below for help.

When you (1) _____ your learning efforts effectively, you (2) _____ the time needed to (3) _____ results. By now you should be well (4) _____ in the managing of prefixes. You've been (5) _____ to mnemonics. That has to make your learning more (6) _____. Notice how much easier it is to make accurate (7) _____ about word meanings. You can (8) _____ additional information from context, adding still further to the (9) _____ of your efforts. Exercises such as this one are indeed (10) _____ to progress.

educe, ducat, duchy, reduce, deduct, seduce, duchess, conduct, produce, educated, ductible, conducive, reproduce, introduced, deductions, productive, abducted, productiveness

(Answers on page 258.)

25

MITTERE

1. When the three-letter sign of the infinitive is
   dropped from *mittere*, "to send," the base form ____
   remains.

   mitt

2. In English words derived from *mittere*, look for the
   idea of "sending." For example, the radio on the
   ship kept "sending" out or trans_____ an SOS
   signal.

   trans*mitting*

3. Or when your car is "sending" out smoke through
   the exhaust you can say it is e_____ smoke.

   e*mitting*

4. If you decide to attend a play you must first buy a
   ticket ad_____ you to the theater to see the
   performance.

   ad*mitting*

intermittent

5. If a sound is sent periodically, starting and stopping at intervals, it is not continuous but inter_____ent.

committee

6. When a group is "sent" to work together on some matter, you ordinarily call them a com_____.

committed

7. Suffixes change words. If you agree to complete this assignment, you have to "send" yourself through it. We say you have com_____ yourself to do it.

admit

8. Of course, sometimes a *t* is dropped off the *mitt* to give us the variant *mit,* as in the phrase you might see on a ticket—"_____ one."

send

9. Since *mittere* means "to send" and *ad-* means "to," *admit* means literally "____ to."

omit

10. If you forget something or neglect to do it, you can be said to o____ it.

submit

11. When you yield to another you literally "send yourself under," or sub____ yourself to another's wishes.

remit

12. After you receive a bill, you send money back for payment, or re____ the money.

permit

13. If you consent to something or allow it, you can be said to per____ it.

admission

14. Again, let your knowledge of English lead you to an important variant form. You would not say "the admit price was high" but that "the ad_____ price was high."

15. If the United States "sends" out an agent or mes-
senger on some specific mission, that person is
called our e_____ary.

    *e*miss*ary*

16. When a painter agrees to paint a certain picture, we
say the painter is com_____ to do it.

    com*missioned*

17. Someone sent on a mission by the church to preach
in a foreign country is called a _____.

    missionary

18. That part of your car which transmits force from
the engine to the wheels is called the t_____-
____.

    transmission

19. If you are careless or negligent at work, or if you
hold back from doing what you should, you are
called re_____.

    re*miss*

20. A weapon designed to be "sent" by throwing or
shooting is appropriately called a m_____.

    m*issile*

21. With the variant *miss*, the final *s* is sometimes
dropped and replaced by an *e*, as in the word
*pro*_____.

    pro*mise*

22. Now put your knowledge of roots to work. As a
definition of *missive*, consider which of the following is closest to the idea of "sending."

    a letter   an error
    a magnet   a heavy object

    a letter

23. With the action "send" in mind, you would infer
that the strange word *remise* probably means

    to judge   to surrender
    to hesitate   to stop.

    to surrender

to set free

24. You would infer that *manumit* probably means

to cut or sever   to light

to injure   to set free or send away.

25. Now when you see a *mitt, mit, miss, mis,* or *mise,* you have strong reason to suspect a word derived from the useful Latin verb *mittere,* meaning "to

send   ____."

Mittere Review Exercise

Fill in the numbered blanks in the following brief context with words derived from *mittere.* Use the list below for help.

By this time, you're not (1) _____ roots to memory. You're using mnemonic aids. Also, you're still reviewing prefixes. (2) _____ me to suggest a way of doing both together. See what prefixes you can add to <u>mittere</u>. Don't (3) _____ you can't think of any and don't (4) ____ any. (5) _____ the list of twenty prefixes to close inspection. Make (6) _____ use of the dictionary. It often (7) _____ additional important information. (8) ____ a sigh or so as you work. That's sure to help. Finally, when you finish, (9) _____ not to (10) _____ <u>mittere</u> from your thoughts as you start the next chapter.

omit, emit, admit, remit, permit, commit, submit, remiss, demise, promise, mission, dismiss, missile, surmise, transmits, compromise, committing, intermittent, submissively

(Answers on page 258.)

Review Test V

A. In the blank after each root in the left-hand column, write the number, from the right-hand list, of the common meaning of the root. The same meaning may apply to more than one root. Some meanings will not be used at all.

1. *capere*	_____	1. have, hold
		2. open
2. *ponere*	_____	3. send
		4. take, seize
3. *tenere*	_____	5. stretch
		6. put, place
4. *ducere*	_____	7. lead
		8. bring
5. *mittere*	_____	

B. From each group of words, select the one word whose meaning is most like that of one of the roots in section A. Enter the appropriate number in the blank at the right.

1. (1) capsize; (2) capacity; (3) capillary; (4) caper   1. _____

2. (1) posture; (2) posse; (3) posterior; (4) possible   2. _____

3. (1) tenth; (2) tennis; (3) tenderize; (4) tenant   3. _____

4. (1) conduct; (2) duplicate; (3) dunce; (4) duckling   4. _____

5. (1) missive; (2) mitten; (3) missus; (4) misspell   5. _____

C. Note the phrase in quotation marks in each sentence and express the same idea with a word containing a form of one of the roots in section A.

1. "Take out," as in the sentence, "All went home _____ _____ Bill."

2. "Put down," as in "_____ your money in the nearest bank."

3. "Hold back," as in "Will you _____ the same classification when you go to the other college?"

4. "Lead in," as in "The government will _____ more men in the next draft call."

5. "Send out," as in "The car was _____ smoke from the exhaust."

(Answers on page 258.)

Verbal Analogy Review Test

Now that you have taken a look at the most common types of relationships used in verbal analogy tests, work through this test to get added experience and to review the relationships. (Answers on page 258.)

1. PREDICAMENT : CARELESSNESS :: RESPONSE :   (1) answer; (2) stimulus; (3) correct; (4) evil.   1. _____

2. REVERT : REVERSION :: SYMPATHIZE : (1) sympathetic; (2) sympathy; (3) symposium; (4) sympathetically.   2. _____

3. DISLOYAL : FAITHLESS :: IMPERFECTION :   (1) depression; (2) praise; (3) defect; (4) pollution.   3. _____

4. CONTEMPORARY : PRESENT :: POSTERITY :   (1) past; (2) present; (3) future; (4) universal.   4. _____

5. ACUTE : CHRONIC :: INTENSE :   (1) beautiful; (2) ill; (3) tonic; (4) persistent.   5. _____

6. ELEGANCE : LUXURY :: POVERTY :   (1) insufficiency; (2) hunger; (3) illness; (4) poorhouse.   6. _____

7. ARTIFICE : FINESSE :: INEPT :   (1) incompetent; (2) skilled; (3) tricky; (4) artistic.   7. _____

8. PROFIT : SELLING :: FAME :   (1) buying; (1) saving; (3) bravery; (4) loving.   8. _____

9. ABIDE : DEPART :: REMAIN :   (1) stay; (2) repair; (3) play; (4) leave.

9. _____

10. BOLD : TIMID :: ADVANCE :   (1) proceed; (2) retreat; (3) run; (4) soldiers.

10. _____

11. PRETTY : UGLY :: ATTRACT :   (1) find; (2) repel; (3) tempt; (4) draw.

11. _____

12. ESTABLISH : BEGIN :: ABOLISH :   (1) enslave; (2) injure; (3) hasten; (4) end.

12. _____

13. INTELLIGENCE : UNDERSTANDING :: STUPIDITY :   (1) ignorance; (2) pleasure; (3) education; (4) unhappiness.

13. _____

14. REMUNERATIVE : PROFITABLE :: FRAUDULENT :   (1) spying; (2) slander; (3) fallacious; (4) rewarding.

14. _____

15. ABSENCE : PRESENCE :: STABLE :   (1) horse; (2) safe; (3) tight; (4) changeable.

15. _____

16. IMMIGRANT : ARRIVAL :: EMIGRANT : (1) departure; (2) flight; (3) alienation; (4) native.

16. _____

17. ADUMBRATE : FORESHADOW :: DECLINE :   (1) increase; (2) decrease; (3) enclose; (4) stupefy.

17. _____

18. DICHOTOMY : DIVISION :: DISSEMBLE : (1) hide; (2) assemble; (3) resemble; (4) reflect.

18. _____

19. DENIGRATE : DEFAMER :: MEDIATE :   (1) statistician; (2) arbitrator; (3) employer; (4) worker.

19. _____

20. OBSTRUCT : IMPEDE :: IMPENETRABLE : (1) long lasting; (2) hidden; (3) impervious; (4) merciful.

20. _____

26

SCRIBERE

write

1. To remember that *scribere* means "to write," associate it with the common word *describe*, which means "to _____ down information about a person or thing."

describing

2. The dictionary definition of *describe* is "to tell or write about." As a better mnemonic, visualize a famous "writer" vividly de_____ some unusual character.

scrib

3. As might be expected, the most common form of *scribere* is found by dropping the *-ere*, leaving the base form _____.

scribe

4. For a word that means "writer," "clerk," "penman," or "secretary," add an *e* to the preceding base form to make the word _____.

176

5. If you "write" carelessly or illegibly, we say you
   _____ble.

   *scrib*ble

6. If you "write" your name at the end of a paper to
   indicate support or approval, you are said to sub-
   _____ to the proposition.

   sub*scribe*

7. When some words or letters are written or engraved
   into a metal plate, we say they are in_____ on it.

   in*scribed*

8. When a secretary puts shorthand notes into readable English, we say they are tran_____.

   tran*scribed*

9. If an old play is thought to be "written" by a certain author, we say it is attributed or a_____ to
   that writer.

   a*scribed*

10. You should now be alerted to *scribere* and its mean-
    ing "to _____."

    write

11. Now use your knowledge of English to bring you to
    a common variant. You do not say, "Give me a
    describtion," but you say, "Give me a de_____-
    ____."

    de*scription*

12. If that description is vivid, it is probably because
    you made use of some good _____ive terms.

    de*script*ive

13. What word originally meant anything "written" but
    now usually refers to the Bible? Think of the rela-
    tionship between *feat* and *feature* to get from *script*
    to _____.

    scripture

14. Another slightly variant form is derived by drop-
    ping the final *t* in *script* to get _____.

    scrip

scriv

15. The last variant form to note is found by substituting a *v* for the *p* in *scrip* to get the form _____.

write

16. With *scrib*, *script*, *scrip*, and *scriv* in mind, you have the necessary information to spot words derived from *scribere*, "to _____."

writing room

17. Now apply that knowledge. You would expect a scriptorium to be a

reading room   writing room
warehouse   waiting room.

copyist

18. And even without a dictionary you would expect a scrivener to be a

file clerk   receptionist
copyist   metal worker.

copy

19. In taking a vocabulary test, if you came to *rescript*, which choice would you select?

request   copy
repeat   TV rerun

to publish

20. In ancient Rome, *proscribe* probably meant

to publish
to announce
to resist.

certificate

21. A *scrip* is probably a

pill   merchant
certificate   screen
                  scout.

super*script*

22. When you write x^2 the 2 is called an exponent or super_____.

23. Before you buy certain pills, you must have a doctor's _____ to take to the drug store to be filled.

prescription

24. When you finish a letter, then "write" an afterthought below your signature, that is called a "P.S." or _____.

postscript

25. A compulsory enrollment of persons into the armed forces is called a con_____ion.

con*script*ion

26. Be sure to cultivate habits of generalizing. If *circumvent* means "to come (*venire*) around (*circum-*)," *circumscribe* means literally "to _____ _____."

write around

27. In the dictionary definition for *circumscribe*, "to trace a line around or limit," the word closest in meaning to *write* is the word _____.

trace

28. Now you can see how helpful the Latin verb _____ "to write," is in dealing with English words.

scribere

29. The variants *scrib, script, scrip,* and the less common *scriv* are the variant forms to look for from the Latin verb _____.

scribere

<u>Scribere</u> Review Exercise

Fill in the numbered blanks in the following brief context with words derived from *scribere*. Use the list below for help.

Here's the (1) _____ for your review of <u>scribere</u>. Just (2) _____ your answers in the numbered blanks. The actual act of writing the answers in this text plays an important role in learning. It's no longer necessary to (3) _____ exactly what you should do here or (4) _____ how to do it. You know. You know you don't have to (5) _____ this exercise on another sheet, as a (6) _____, or put it in typed (7) _____ form, with a personal (8) _____ on the cover. But you do have to (9) _____ to certain learning procedures, such as writing in the answers. No (10) _____ is needed to that.

script, scribe, ascribe, rescript, describe, scribble, proscribe, scripture, prescribe, subscribe, ascription, manuscript, postscript, transcribe, nondescript, inscription

(Answers on page 258.)

27

FACERE

1. It takes a skilled word detective to identify *facere*, "to make or do," in all its variant forms. Drop the *-ere* to get the important base form ___.

fac

2. An exact reproduction—"made" similar to the original—would appropriately be called a ___-simile.

*fac*simile

3. If the workers show real skill and speed, they can be called ___ile workers.

facile

4. A facile craftsman is one who "does" things with genuine ___ility.

facility

fact

5. If you are talking about something that is true or was actually "done," just add a *t* to the base form to make the word ____, a variant of *facere*.

factory

6. A building in which things are manufactured, or "made," is sometimes called a _____.

benefactor

7. If *bene-* means "good" or "well," a person who helps, often giving financial assistance, is known as a _____.

manu*factures*

8. If a company "makes" cars, we say it manu____-____ them.

fac

9. What letters do the variants *fac*, *fact*, and *factur* have in common?

make

10. Just as *run* and *ran* are forms of the same verb, so *fac* and *fic* are both forms of *facere*, "to ____ or do."

efficacious

11. Which of the following words probably contains a form of *facere*?
efficacious   fabulous
flaccid   finesse

fice

12. Try to generalize about *facere* from your knowledge of *scribere*. If you know that *scrib* and *scribe* are variants of *scribere*, you should expect *fic* and ____ to be variants of *facere*.

trick

13. Using your root knowledge, in which choice is "making" or "doing" dominant? An *artifice* is a
necklace   trick
tall plant   artery.

14. Judging from the *fice*, an *edifice* is probably a
tree	opening
wind	building.

building

15. The change of vowel from *fac* to *fic* suggests that *fec* might also be a variant form of _____.

facere

16. Think of a word with *fec*. A blemish or flaw is, for example, often spoken of as an imper_____.

imper*fection*

17. *Imperfection* is the condition of not being _____ perfectly, more evidence that the word is derived from the Latin verb _____.

made
facere

18. With root meaning in mind, if you read about an efficacious drug you can see reason for thinking of it as
costly	effective
weak	harmful.

effective

19. At first sight you might not expect *fash* to be a variant until you think of a _____ionable article — an article "made" to be in style.

*fash*ionable

20. You would expect *feat* to be another variant, since an "act or deed of an unusual nature" is actually called a _____.

feat

21. Now change the *t* in *feat* to *s* and add *ible*. If something can be "done," it is indeed _____.

feasible

22. Do not overlook *fit* as still another variant. When someone "does" well by you, it is a real bene____.

bene*fit*

counter*feit*

23. That still does not exhaust the possible variants. A bogus ten-dollar bill is not "made" by the government and is not real money but counter_____ money.

fect

24. Always corroborate inferences about derivation by checking both form and meaning. In the word *defect*, the letters ____ look like a form from *facere*.

made

25. Checking the meaning of the word, you see that an article with a *defect* is not ____ perfectly.

dictionary

26. Your final authoritative check on this and other derivations should be made by consulting your desk _____.

*mak*ing

27. Whenever you see a *fac, fact, fic, feat, feas, featur,* or *fair*, look for the idea of ___ing or doing.

Facere Review Exercise

Fill in the numbered blanks in the following brief context with words derived from *facere*. Use the listing below for help.

"Making" and "doing" rank so high for us that <u>facere</u> (1) _____ our language with more than usual frequency. In (2) ____, it will be (3) _____ clear from the listing below that <u>facere</u> is indeed a very (4) _____ shortcut. It would also be (5) _____ to find a root with more variant forms. The most noticeable (6) _____ of words derived from <u>facere</u> is the letter <u>f</u>. If you're to be really (7) _____ in spotting <u>facere</u> words, look for an <u>f</u> followed by an <u>a</u>, <u>e</u>, or <u>i</u>. That should (8) _____ your analysis. An added (9) _____ is the idea of "making" or "doing." If a company "makes" or (10) _____ _____ baseballs, and you see an <u>fa</u> in the word along with the idea of "making," you're almost sure to have a word from <u>facere</u>.

feat, fact, factor, affair, defect, perfect, benefit, factory, affects, fashion, faculty, feature, faction, perfectly, effective, difficult, defective, efficient, infection, facsimile, proficient, facilitate, artificial, benefactor, forfeiture, confection, imperfection, inefficiency, disaffection, unification, manufactures

(Answers on page 258.)

28

TENDERE

stretch

1. *Tendere* means "to stretch." Whenever you suspect a derivative of that Latin verb, be sure to look for the meaning "to _____."

tend

2. *Tendere* has only three important variant forms. The first is found by dropping the three-letter infinitive ending to give us the base form ____.

attention

3. Your knowledge of English will lead easily to the other two. When you attend class, you must give things your full at____ion.

extension

4. And when you extend credit to someone, that ex____ion of credit is important.

186

5. Now you have all three variants — *tend, tent,* and *tens.* What three letters do they all have in common? ___

ten

6. Remember the Latin verb *tenere,* "to have or hold"? When you drop the infinitive ending you have ____.

ten

7. Note a significant difference. When *ten* is followed by a *d, t,* or *s,* it is probably from *tendere,* "to _____."

stretch

8. Unfortunately one variant of *tenere* is *tent,* a form identical with a variant from _____, meaning "to stretch."

tendere

9. To resolve such confusions, you must rely heavily on meaning. For example, a piece of canvas "stretched" so as to provide a shelter is called a ____.

tent

10. In which of the following words is the idea of "holding" or "having" dominant?
    retention   attend
    extend

retention

11. In which of the following words is the idea of "stretching" predominant?
    retention   attend
    extend

extend

12. An added silent *e* to *tens* should not confuse you. If you stretch your muscles tight they are no longer relaxed but _____.

tense

*tens*ion

13. Mental or nervous strain, often with muscular tautness, is spoken of as ____ion.

tensile

14. A wire that can stand a good bit of pull or "stretch" is said to have high _____ strength.

*tend*ency

15. If there is an inclination or disposition toward something, we call it a ____ency in that direction.

tend

16. If you have a tendency to do your best work in the morning, we can say that you ____ to work best at that time.

intend

17. When you have a plan or purpose in mind — literally, when you "stretch" yourself "in" a certain direction — you can be said to _____ to do something.

intention

18. And when you intend to do something, that becomes your _____.

*superintend*ent

19. Someone who supervises a group is often called a _____ent.

*pretend*ing

20. When I claim something falsely or simulate illness, I am said to be _____ing.

stretch

21. When you *pretend* to be something you aren't, you use a word which means, literally, "to _____ before."

at*tend*

22. When you "stretch" yourself to class, you are said to at____ class.

23. When you struggle with difficulties—literally
    "stretch together" with them—you have to con____
    with them.

    con*tend*

24. Judging from root knowledge, if I am ostentatious,
    I am probably

    quiet   young
    short   big-headed.

    big-headed

25. In defining *subtend*, which choice is most strongly
    related to the idea of "stretching"?

    place under
    extend under
    press under

    extend under

26. If a sack is distended it is probably

    flattened   small
    swollen   brown
                 close-woven.

    swollen

27. When you see a *tend, tent,* or *tens* in a word, suspect
    the meaning, "to _____."

    stretch

<u>Tendere</u> Review Exercise

Fill in the numbered blanks in the following brief context with words derived from *tendere*. Use the list below for help.

Anything which makes words more interesting to you (1) _____ to (2) _____ your vocabulary. (3) _____ to derivation has that effect, we (4) _____. At least that's the (5) _____. If you only (6) _____ interest, you lose out. Take the word, <u>pretend</u>. Look at the word (7) _____ and you see that it means literally "to stretch" (<u>tendere</u>) "before" (<u>pre-</u>). What a vivid picture—the real you hiding behind a false face you stretched before. Such a picture certainly has a (8) _____ to heighten interest. So, your (9) _____ efforts (10) _____ increased interest and improved results.

tent, tense, tends, tendon, extend, extent, tensile, tension, contend, pretend, portend, subtend, portent, distend, tendency, intently, pretense, extensive, intention, attention, pretender, ostentation, superintend.

(*Answers on page 259.*)

29

SPECERE

1. The Latin verbs *specere*, *spectare*, and *spicere* have one thing in common: they all mean "to see or look," as in our word *spectator*—one who ____ or _____.

sees
looks

2. Three of the most important forms to look for are found by dropping the infinitive ending from *specere*, *spectare*, and *spicere* to get the base forms ____, _____, and ____.

spec
spect
spic

3. Use your root knowledge to put ideas across more succinctly. For example, to "look into" matters carefully, as in examining items prior to shipping, would be to _____ them.

inspect

4. Here is a chance to apply your knowledge of pre-

fixes. Think of the prefix meaning "out." When you are awaiting someone—literally "looking out" for him—you say you _____ him any minute.

expect

5. When you progress you "step forward." When you retrogress, you "step back." Now as you "look back," your childhood days may seem happy and carefree in retro_____.

retro*spect*

6. In your present position, as you "look ahead," you might say the _____ for advancement are good.

prospects

7. If the *circumference* is the distance "around" a circle, when you "look around" carefully before acting, you are rightly called _____ in your behavior.

circumspect

8. *Extro-* and *intro-* are opposites. If an extrovert is one more interested in others than in himself, one primarily interested in himself would be called an _____.

introvert

9. An introvert tends to "look within" himself at his own feelings and reactions, a process known as intro_____ion.

intro*spect*ion

10. When you have an especially good vantage point for looking things over, for seeing through problems, we say your per_____ive is good.

per*spect*ive

11. If someone deserves your esteem or regard and is someone you can "look" to "again and again," you are said to _____ that person.

respect

12. If you know the prefix meaning "to" or "toward," you can add it to *spect* to get the word that fits this context: "I'm not well acquainted with all parts, or _____, of the business."

aspects

13. One who paints is a painter. In the same way, that which is a "visible" disembodied spirt or ghost may be called a _____.

specter

14. Looking back at *specere* and *spectare,* we see that dropping the infinitive endings leaves two forms; the only difference between them is the letter _.

t

15. So far we have looked at words with *spect.* Drop the *t* for the word that fits the following context. When you collect samples of something, you can speak of them as ____imens.

*spec*imens

16. Roots are invaluable in leading you to meaning. Take the strange word *speculum.* Root knowledge should let you know that it means.
    speech   bill
    charm   mirror.

mirror

17. When someone talks about *specious* reasoning, you will note *spec* and infer that this kind of reasoning
    is subtle   is right
    looks right but isn't   seems involved.

looks right
but isn't

18. People who "watch" games, programs, and the like are known as _____.

spectators

19. Think of the prefix meaning "under" to get the next word. With certain individuals, when you tend

suspect

to "look" beneath or "under" outward appearances,
you are said to distrust or _____ them.

spic

20. All the English derivatives of the Latin verbs meaning "to see or look" that we have studied so far
have contained *spec.* If you drop the infinitive ending from *spicere,* you have _____.

suspicion

21. Actually your knowledge of English would bring
you to *spic.* You would not say you look on him
with suspicion but with _____.

despise

22. When you descend you go "down." When you
"look down" on people with contempt or scorn,
you _____ them.

*despic*able

23. A character who deserves to be despised is called a
_____able character.

*despicab*ly

24. One who behaves in a despicable manner behaves
_____ly.

au*spices*

25. If a sponsoring agent or agency is "seeing" to some
of the details of a program, we can say it is given
under their au_____.

spy

26. If I "look" around secretly and furtively to get
valuable military information, I am probably a ____.

clear-sighted

27. You now have another key to unlock word meanings. If you are perspicacious, you are probably
clear-sighted   intelligent
obvious   hot.

28. By now, a *spec* or *spic* should make you think of the
meanings "to look or ___."   see

Specere Review Exercise

Fill in the numbered blanks in the following brief context with
words derived from *specere*. Use the list below for help.

These context-root exercises are designed to help you develop
(1) _____ (2) _____ with words. You can (3) _____ to be
able to use prefix and root knowledge with increasing skill, a (4)
_____ to be welcomed. In (5) _____, you can see what
(6) _____ gains you've made. You have established that all-
important habit of (7) _____ words carefully, with the (8)
_____ of discovering known word-part (9) _____. In
that (10) _____ you're becoming much more knowledgeable.

*spy, aspect, expect, espial, specify, special, respect, prospect, specious,
specimens, retrospect, despicable, auspicious, inspecting, spectacles,
respective, expectation, prospective, respectable, circumspect, per-
spicacity*

(*Answers on page 259.*)

30

PLICARE

plic

1. The Latin verb *plicare*, "to fold," has more variant forms than most verbs. To find the obvious one, drop the infinitive ending to get the base form _____.

plicat

2. The verb in Latin also appears in the form *plicatus*. Dropping the *-us* ending gives you another important form, _____.

plicit

3. To find still a third form, change the *a* in *plicat* to *i*, making _____.

plic

4. What letters do the three variants *plic*, *plicat*, and *plicit* have in common? _____

pli

5. Sometimes even the *c* is dropped and you have the variant ___ remaining.

6. Now work through the next items to familiarize yourself with these forms. When you fold a sheet of paper together several times, you make it more difficult or com_____ to read.

com*plicated*

7. By this time you are accustomed to seeing a silent *e* added to some base forms. For example, a partner in crime goes by the special name of an accom-_____.

accom*plice*

8. If some plastic is "foldable" you can also speak of it as ___able.

*pli*able

9. We say it is not what was said but what was intimated or im_____ that is most important.

im*plied*

10. When what one says involves others, we say it im_____ them in the crime also.

im*plicated*

11. When you make something clear or "unfold" all the details, you are said to explain or ex_____ it.

ex*pli*cate

12. When something is said clearly and distinctly, we say it was stated definitely or ex_____.

ex*plicitly*

13. When you beg humbly, you literally "fold" yourself "under," or become a sup_____ant.

sup*pli*cant

14. The change from *i* to *y* in *pli* opens up a whole new subfamily, as illustrated in ___*wood*.

*ply*wood

15. Add the prefix meaning "together" to *ply* to make a word meaning to "act in accord with a request, de-

comply

mand, order, or rule," as to _____ with the new regulations.

16. Let your knowledge of English suggest still another variant. If directions are complicated, they are involved or com____.

com*plex*

17. The color, texture, and general appearance of your skin, particularly of your face, is spoken of as your com_____.

com*plexion*

18. Because the body was originally thought to be a "folding together" of four humors, it was considered complex, hence the word *com_____*.

com*plexion*

19. These next variants are not so frequently found but are still useful shortcuts. With *pli*, change the *i* to *e* as you think of a word describing an individual who is limber and flexible, a sup___ individual.

• sup*ple*

20. This variant helps you define *duple* as meaning

two-fold

    durable   sensible
    stupid   two-fold
                two-faced.

21. A flat double "fold" in cloth or other material is called a _____ (rhymes with *eat*), still another variant.

pleat

22. *Plait* is another variant. When you plait some material you

pleat it

    pleat it   sew it
    wear it   weave it.

23. Still another variant is found in the word meaning,

literally, "to fold apart," or exhibit to advantage, as
in a show window where goods are placed on dis-
____.   dis*play*

24. In addition to *pli*, *ple*, and *pla*, there is *ploy*. When
you use several people to complete a job, probably
paying them, you can be said to em____ them.   em*ploy*

25. And in a military operation, when troops are spread
out, we say they are de____ed.   de*ploy*ed

26. Now you have been introduced to the multi____ity
of forms to be noted for *plicare*.   multi*plic*ity

27. It is quite a step from *multiplicity* to its opposite—
freedom from complexity, or sim_____.   sim*plicity*

28. Now you are ready to deal more effectively with the
hundreds of words derived from *plicare*, meaning
"to ____."   fold

<u>Plicare</u> **Review Exercise**

Fill in the numbered blanks in the following brief context with words derived from *plicare*. Use the list below for help if needed.

Knowing prefix and root meanings is not enough. The payoff step is to be able to (1) _____ that knowledge. Obviously that's not a (2) _____ but often quite a (3) _____ matter. Since you know many techniques to (4) _____, it's easier for you, however. Proper (5) _____ will (6) _____ the accuracy of your analysis of words. Remember also to (7) _____ with the demands of the pro-grammed form. Each frame demands an (8) _____ answer. Take a closer look at <u>explicit</u>, literally "to fold out," a fascinating word pic-ture. Fold a typed sheet several times; then try to read it. You can't—until it's "folded out." Extra meaning and interest are (9) _____ in that picture. (10) _____ such word pictures to bring words to life.

reply, apply, imply, plait, deploy, plexus, pliant, employ, supple, comply, simple, duplex, pliable, complex, display, simplify, explicit, implicit, employer, employee, multiply, complication, application

(Answers on page 259.)

31

STARE

1. The Latin verb *stare* means "to stand." When you drop the *-re,* you have the form common to most English derivatives, the base form ___.

   sta

2. If you like to travel to lands that "stand" far away, you prefer far-off places and di_____ lands.

   di*stant*

3. Out on the golf course, when you are about to address the ball, you take your "stand" or, as we more frequently say, your _____.

   stance

4. If a person "stands" firm in purpose and steady in loyalties, we call him con_____.

   con*stant*

5. When a country is given permanent organization—

established

is "stood" on its feet, so to speak — we say it is
founded or e_ _ _ blished.

6. When you add *ex-* to *stant*, the *x* already ends in an *s*
sound, so you drop the *s* in *stant* to make *ex_ _ _ _*,
which means still standing or existing — not lost or
destroyed — as an old manuscript.

extant

7. If something "stands" in your way or obstructs
progress we call it an ob_ _ _ _ _ _.

obstacle

8. When people are brought to trial, they are seldom
judged on circum_ _ _ _ _ _ _ _ evidence only.

circumstantial

9. A circumstance is a factor attending an act, event,
or condition. Circumstantial evidence is, therefore,
evidence surrounding that act — literally "_ _ _ _ _ ing
around (*circum-*)" it.

standing

10. Our word *status*, meaning "standing" or "rank,"
comes from Latin directly into English without
change; it is another principal part of *stare*, meaning "to _ _ _ _ _."

stand

11. Dropping the *-us* ending in *status* gives you another
important variant form to look for, the form _ _ _ _.

stat

12. This form is found in many English words. The terminal or "standing" place for trains and buses is
called a _ _ _ _ ion.

station

13. When a train moves into the station and stops, it is
then not moving, or is _ _ _ _ _ _ _ _ _ _.

stationary

14. A piece of sculpture "standing" on a pedestal is usually spoken of as a _____.

statue

15. If I am restored to my old position or state, you can say I was rein_____.

rein*stated*

16. Still another variant comes from the related verb form *sistere,* meaning "to cause to stand." Dropping the three-letter sign of the infinitive leaves the base form ____.

sist

17. This form opens up countless other possibilities. If protestors demand their rights, "standing" firm "in" those demands, we say they _____ on their rights.

insist

18. If, despite all kinds of opposition, you continue to press forward on your course, we say you are per_____.

per*sistent*

19. If thieves "stand back" in an attempt to elude capture by police officers, we say they are re_____ arrest.

re*sisting*

20. Now think of the prefix that means "to" or "toward." Add it to *sist* to get the word that means to help someone do something—in other words, to _____ someone.

assist

21. If you take the prefix meaning "together," and add it to a form of *stare,* you get a word meaning "made up of or composed of certain parts"—the word _____.

consist

22. In a few words the root is *sti* or *st* instead of *sta* or

armi*stice*

sist, as in the word describing the stopping or "standing still" of armed hostilities—the word *armi*_____.

sol*stice*

23. The same form is used when talking about the time of year when the sun reaches the farthest point from the equator, north or south—the sol_____.

substitute

24. When something happens to a regular teacher so he is not able to meet his classes, another is sometimes "stood" in his place—a _____ teacher.

stands

25. If a platform is stable, your knowledge of roots will remind you that it _____ firmly in place.

stand

26. Be on the alert from now on for *sta, stat, sti,* and *sist*—all suggesting the meaning "to _____."

Stare Review Exercise

Fill in the numbered blanks in the following brief context with words derived from *stare*. Use the list below for help.

If, despite (1) _____, you (2) _____ in your efforts, you'll see (3) _____ gains when you finish this text. Exercises of this kind will (4) _____ you. Don't (5) _____ when you're progressing so nicely. You have only a short (6) _____ yet to go. Although growth is seldom (7) _____, you're definitely moving ahead, not standing (8) _____. These exercises provide strong (9) _____ in (10) _____ improved word power.

exist, desist, assist, arrest, estate, consist, restate, instant, persist, constant, contrast, distance, instance, obstacles, destitute, armistice, establish, constitute, stationary, assistance, substantial, consistency, restitution, establishing, irresistible, circumstance

(*Answers on page 259.*)

Review Test VI

A. In the blank after each root in the left-hand column, write the number, from the right-hand list, of the common meaning of the root. The same meaning may apply to more than one root. Some meanings will not be used at all.

1. *scribere*	_____	1. speak
		2. see
2. *facere*	_____	3. write
3. *tendere*	_____	4. have, hold
		5. fold
4. *specere*	_____	6. make, do
		7. press
5. *plicare*	_____	8. stretch

B. From each group of words, select the one word whose meaning is most like that of one of the roots in section A. Enter the appropriate number in the blank at the right.

1. (1) scribble; (2) scrimmage; (3) scrimp; (4) sculpture   1. _____

2. (1) face; (2) manufacture; (3) fade; (4) failure   2. _____

3. (1) tenor; (2) tenpins; (3) extend; (4) tempo   3. _____

4. (1) special; (2) speedy; (3) speech; (4) spectator   4. _____

5. (1) plod; (2) pliant; (3) plural; (4) plunge   5. _____

Note the phrase in quotation marks in each sentence and express the same idea with a word containing a form of one of the roots in section A.

1. "Write down" as in the sentence, "Did you read his graphic _____ of the leading character?"

2. "Able to be done" as in the sentence, "His plan was the most _____ of all."

3. "Stretch to" as in "He will _____ every one of the meetings."

4. "See into" as in "Do you want to _____ the finished product?"

5. "Fold in" as in "It was not so much what he said as what he _____ that bothered me."

(*Answers on page 259.*)

32

FERRE (latus)

1. Take the Latin verb *ferre* and drop the last two letters to get the base form most often found in English, the form ___.

   fer

2. Remembering that a common meaning of *re-* is "back," if *refer* means literally "to bear or carry back," you would infer that *ferre* means "to ____ or _____."

   bear
   carry

3. *Ferre* is an irregular verb with *latus* as one of its forms. Drop the *-us* ending from *latus* to get the other important form in English, the form ___.

   lat

4. With *lat*, do not overlook the possibility of a silent *e*, bringing you to an even more common form, as in the English word *re____*, which means to "carry back" or tell.

   re*late*

207

referee

5. In a football or basketball game, the person to whom matters are "carried" or referred for decision is called a re_____.

ferry

6. A boat designed to "carry" passengers over a narrow body of water is called a _____ boat.

coniferous

7. A cone-bearing tree is technically known as a coni___ous tree.

pestiferous

8. In the same way, *pest-bearing* becomes, in a word, *pesti*_____.

ferre

9. Watch out for possible confusion between the Latin noun *ferrum*, meaning "iron," and the Latin verb _____, meaning "to bear or carry."

iron-bearing

10. Strangely enough both roots are found in a single word—*ferriferous*. Your root knowledge should help you define a ferriferous rock as an _____-_____ rock.

i

11. As you can see, often an extra letter is inserted between two roots to bring them together into a single word. In *ferriferous* as in *pestiferous* it is the letter _.

vociferous

12. Try some word coining of your own. If *vocare* is a Latin verb meaning "to call," the word meaning clamorous or "noise-bearing" would probably be ___i_____.

flower-bearing

13. This should prepare you nicely for such technical words as *floriferous*, which you would assume to mean

thorn-bearing   flower-bearing
leaf-bearing   fruit-bearing.

14. And you would infer that *fructiferous* probably means

    leaf-bearing
    fruit-bearing
    thorn-bearing.

    fruit-bearing

15. If soil produces abundant crops and is rich in nutrients, it is appropriately spoken of as ＿＿tile.

    *fer*tile

16. When two people get together to talk over matters, we say they con＿＿＿ about them.

    con*fer*

17. If you "carry" into what you read certain things that lie between the lines, you are said to be making in＿＿＿＿＿＿＿＿.

    in*fer*ences

18. During a church service, a collection, or an ＿＿-＿＿＿＿＿＿ is usually taken up.

    *offer*ing

19. If you are literally "borne under" by pain, you are said to suf＿＿＿ pain.

    suf*fer*

20. If you remember that *dis-* means "apart," when two people are "carried apart" by their conflicting views, we say that they ＿＿＿＿＿＿.

    dif*fer*

21. Now for the other basic form, *lat* (or *late*). If you "carry" ideas across from one language to another, it is called trans＿＿＿ing.

    trans*lat*ing

22. When you speak of something in exaggerated terms, with more enthusiasm than usual, you probably use super＿＿＿＿＿＿＿.

    super*latives*

compare them

23. Judging from root meaning, when you correlate sets of figures, you probably
    list them   compare them.
    add them

elation

24. If you are "carried" out of your usual self by some good news, you are no doubt in a state of e___ion.

relate

25. If you witness an accident and then tell a friend about it, you are said to re____ the story to him.

inferential

26. You would infer from your knowledge of prefix and root elements that *illative* probably means
    opinionated   wishful
    inferential   exhausting.

elongated
(or "carried" out)

27. And a *prolate* spheroid is probably a spheroid that is
    elongated
    irregular
    small.

carry

28. Now whenever you spot a word with either *fer* or *lat* you will know to look for the meaning or idea, "to bear or _____."

Ferre Review Exercise

Fill in the numbered blanks in the following brief context with words derived from *ferre*. Use the list below for help.

To remember that <u>ferre</u> means "to bear or carry," think of a __(1)__—something which bears you over a body of water. ___(2)___ ferre with "ferry" does help you remember the meaning. If a ___(3)___ mnemonic works better for you, fine. Use your own ___(4)___ rather than the one just ___(5)___ above. The important thing is not to __(6)__ or

_(7)_ _ making a useful association. Enjoy the _ _ _(8)_ _ _ of finding one that really works. Don't _ _(9)_ _ failure or _ _(10)_ _ excuses. Just act.

infer, defer, refer, ferry, delay, confer, relate, differ, prefer, suffer, referee, proffer, fertile, offered, elation, transfer, relative, relation, relating, deference, inference, translate, different, coniferous, referendum, sufferance, preference.

(Answers on page 259.)

33

GRAPHEIN

1. In the Latin verb *tenere,* the last three letters indicate the infinitive. In the Greek verb *graphein,* the last three letters also indicate the _____.

infinitive

2. *Graphein* is in the infinitive form. Does it mean "I write" or "to write"?

to write

3. As is the case with most Latin verbs, that part of *graphein* which most frequently comes over into English is found by dropping the infinitive ending to get the form _____.

graph

4. A diagram representing changes by means of a curve or series of bars is spoken of as a _____.

graph

212

5. A host of words are made through suffix additions. For example, the substance in a pencil that does the "writing" is called _____ite.

*graph*ite

6. And if you give us a realistic, vivid description of a scene, it can appropriately be called a graph__ description.

grap*hic*

7. If a monolith is, literally, a "single stone," a "writer in stone" or one who prints from stone plates would be called a litho_____.

litho*grapher*

8. Just as the letter *i* connects *pest* and *ferous* in *pestiferous,* so when adding *lith* to *grapher* we need a letter to make the two parts sound like one word. In this case the connecting letter is the letter _.

o

9. It is possible, in a sense, to "write with light." Using a camera it is possible to take a picture or photo_____ something.

photo*graph*

10. Knowing that *photography* is "light-writing" you can infer that the combining form *photo-* means "_____."

light

11. Today it's possible to "write with sound." We can buy records with "sound-writing" and play them on our own phono_____.

phono*graph*

12. Now you should be able to infer that *phono-* means "_____."

sound

13. Famous people are often plagued by people who want them to sign, or _____, their names.

autograph

orthography

14. If *ortho-* is from a Greek word meaning "straight," writing or spelling words in a correct fashion is the science or subject _____ (rhymes with *geography*).

porno*graphy*

15. Would you expect writing about prostitutes to be obscene? If you know that the Greek word, *porne*, means "prostitute," you know where we got our word porno_____.

lexico*grapher*

16. If our word *lexicon* means "dictionary," you would expect the "writer" of a dictionary to be a lexico_- _____.

pyrographer

17. If a pyromaniac is one with a persistent compulsion to start destructive fires, one skilled in burning design on wood or leather would be a p___- _____.

seismograph

18. If the combining form *seismo* means "earthquake," then an instrument for recording or writing earthquake shocks would be a _____.

typographer

19. In printing, a person skilled in setting, arranging, or writing with type is not called a type grapher but, in a word, a _____.

*topograph*ical

20. If you know that *topos* is a Greek word meaning "place," a survey of some place with all its contours represented would be called a _____ical survey.

chirographer

21. If *chiro-* is a combining form meaning "hand," an expert penman or handwriter would be a _____- _____.

22. If you know that *steno-* means "narrow," you can see why one who records in a narrow space (by shorthand) what is said is called a _____.

stenographer

23. The Greek word *mimos* means "imitator," which suggests why a machine for making imitations or copies of written material is called a _____ machine.

mimeograph

24. If the Greek word *chorein* means "choral dance," the person who designs the movements of a ballet would be the _____.

choreographer

25. Knowledge of English should lead you to the only important variant form of *graph*. A telegraph message is called a tele_____.

tele*gram*

26. In school when you study a language, you usually study the rules for its use or its writing—in other words, its _____.

grammar

27. In reviewing this unit, remember the two most common forms of *graphein* are _____ and ____, meaning "to _____."

graph
gram
write

Graphein Review Exercise

Fill in the numbered blanks in the following brief context with words derived from *graphein*. Use the list below for help.

From the Greek root, <u>graphein</u>, we get mostly long words. When you write a research report, you usually have a (1) _____ at the end. If you're quite famous, people may ask for your (2) _____. If you write a book about someone's life, you become a (3) _____. If your handwriting is beautiful, you may get compli- mented on your (4) _____. If you spell well, your (5) _____ is good. If you take good pictures, you're a good (6) _____. An instrument for recording earthquakes is a (7) _____. If you write dictionaries, you're a (8) _____. If you're able to write shorthand, you're probably a (9) _____. And all those big words are written in one (10) _____.

monograph, autograph, telegraph, paragraph, pyrography, typography, stylograph, biographer, multigraph, lithograph, orthography, seismograph, calligraphy, stenographer, bibliography, photographer, cinematograph, lexicographer

(*Answers on page 260.*)

34

LOGOS

1. What is the best way to remember the three key meanings of the Greek noun *logos*? Try mnemonics as your aid to m_____.

memory

2. Let us start with the original meaning of *logos* — "speech" or "word." Associate this meaning with the word *monologue*, one person making a "speech," or saying _____.

words

3. Another meaning is "reason." To remember this more easily, think of the word suggesting the use of correct reasoning, our word ___*ic*.

*log*ic

4. It is a short step from "reason" to "science of" or "study of," as in geo_____, the study of individual rock types.

geo*logy*

logo

5. For a closer look at variant forms, drop the *s* from *logos* to get the form ____, as found in *logograph,* meaning a kind of word puzzle.

log

6. Now drop the *o* from *logo* to get the even shorter form ___, as in *monolog.*

logue

7. Another, longer spelling of *monolog* brings you to still another variant, the form _____, as in *monologue.*

biology

8. And in many words the form is *logy,* as in the science of bio_____.

logos

9. Knowing the forms *logo, log, logue,* and *logy,* you should now be able to identify the more than 150 English words derived from the Greek noun _____.

philologist

10. If *philein* is a Greek word meaning "love," a "word lover" or "student of words" is appropriately called a philo___ist.

astrology

11. The Greek word *astron* means "star." The so-called "science of" the stars, foretelling their influence on human affairs, is astro_____.

astronaut

12. Going a step farther, if the Greek word *nautes* means "sailor," a "sailor" or navigator in the "stars" would be rightly called an astro_____.

prologue

13. Introductory lines or verses in a play or poem would be called a pro_____.

14. If the word *decade* means a group of "ten," the Ten

Commandments or ten "words" would be called the ____logue.

*deca*logue

15. Two people talking together, as in a play, will give us a dia_____.

dia*logue*

16. A "study of" myths would appropriately be called m_____.

m*ythology*

17. And "words" about travel give us the handy word *t*_____.

tra*velogue*

18. The Greek word *etymon* refers to the literal sense of a word. The "study of" the origin and development of words would, therefore, be called *etymo*____.

etymo*logy*

19. If a euphonious sound is good to listen to, a "speech" of praise would be called a eu_____.

eu*logy*

20. The "study of" crime is known as _____.

criminology

21. In every field there is a special nomenclature that must be mastered—the various technical terms in the field. This is spoken of as the t___inology.

ter*m*inology

22. When you speak of life as being like a river, that type of comparison is called an ana_____.

ana*logy*

23. If *kata* is a Greek word meaning "down" or "completely," a complete "writing" down of all items for sale, as for a mail order house, would be called a ____log.

*cata*log

dramas

24. Thinking in terms of the original meaning of *logos*, you would expect the word *tetralogy* to refer to a series of four

buildings   dramas
pictures   pantomimes.

phrases

25. Judging from the original meaning, *tautology* is apparently a word relating to

customs   desires
phrases   foods.

word

26. A neologism would apparently be a new

conclusion   amount
word   task.

*lex*icon
dia*lect*

27. The noun *logos* comes from the verb *legein*, "to speak," hence the forms *lex* and *lect* as in such words as ___icon and *dia*____.

science

28. In addition to the meanings "speech" and "words," the other two meanings of *logos* to remember are "reason" and "_____ of."

Logos Review Exercise

Fill in the numbered blanks in the following brief context with words derived from *logos*. Use the list below for help.

Think of all the -ology words in the English language. If you're thinking about words, you can make a regular (1) _____ of them. When you study word derivations, you look at their (2) _____. If you're more concerned about how they are put into phrases, that's (3) _____, just as words about religion get into the area of (4) _____. If one person is doing the talking, that's a (5) _____;

if two or more are talking together it's a (6) _____. If it's a love of learning about classical or literary things, it's (7) _____. If it's words spoken before a performance, it's a (8) _____; and if it's words about travel, it's a (9) _____. It all adds up to the kind of (10) _____ we get from <u>logos</u>.

eulogy, analogy, apology, biology, catalog, dialogue, theology, epilogue, prologue, anthology, philology, astrology, monologue, etymology, illogical, archeology, travelogue, chronology, entomology, criminology, phraseology, terminology

(Answers on page 260.)

Review Test VII

A. In the blank after each root in the left-hand column, write the number, from the right-hand list, of the common meaning of the root. The same meaning may apply to more than one root. Some meanings will not be used at all.

1. *stare*	_____	1. discover
		2. calculate
2. *ferre*	_____	3. stand
		4. see
		5. write
3. *graphein*	_____	6. speech, study of
		7. bear, carry
4. *logos*	_____	8. lower

B. From each group of words, select the one word whose meaning is most like that of one of the roots in section A. Enter the appropriate number in the blank at the right.

1. (1) stalk; (2) stay; (3) stagger; (4) star   1. _____

2. (1) infer; (2) ferocious; (3) festival; (4) fever   2. _____

3. (1) grasp; (2) grape; (3) grapple; (4) graffiti   3. _____

4. (1) log; (2) logical; (3) long; (4) lotion   4. _____

C. Note the word or phrase in quotation marks in each sentence and express the same idea with a word containing a form of one of the roots in section A.

1. "Standing," as in the sentence, "He was quite conscious of anything that might affect his _____ in the community."

2. "Carry in," as in the sentence, "He didn't say so exactly, but I _____ that's what he meant."

3. "Self-written," as in the sentence, "I got him to _____ his latest book."

4. "Speaking between," as in the sentence, "The _____ in that play is very witty."

(Answers on page 260.)

Root Mini-Review

To complete this section on the fourteen roots, here's another mini-review. Use your three-by-five-inch card as before. Try whichever of the three patterns seems best for hastening your mastery of these elements.

Root	Suggested Mnemonic	Common Meaning
1. *capere*	capture	take, seize
2. *ponere*	deposit	put, place
3. *tenere*	tenant	have, hold
4. *ducere*	abduct	lead
5. *mittere*	missile	send
6. *scribere*	describe	write
7. *facere*	feat, fashion	make, do
8. *tendere*	tend	stretch
9. *specere*	inspect	see

10. *plicare*	pliant	fold
11. *stare*	stationary	stand
12. *ferre*	ferry	bear, carry
13. *graphein*	autograph	write
14. *logos*	terminology	study of, speech

Repeat whenever necessary for a quick review.

Optional Review Essay (continued)

As with the preceding part of this essay, if you want a faster review, turn again to the short passages on pages 242 and 243. This time, put special emphasis on reviewing roots.

To continue with your review of both prefixes and roots, using this essay, fill in the blanks with the appropriate prefixes. You'll find prefix meanings in the margin, as before. To refresh your mind, you may want to refer to page 142 for a list of the twenty prefixes, and to page 222 for a list of the fourteen roots.

To review the roots, follow a somewhat different procedure. When *you perceive a line marked with an asterisk, you know it contains a word with one of the fourteen roots studied. Using your dictionary, *check until you find the exact word with one of those roots. This *should serve as a graphic reminder of the role of the dictionary in *verifying your hypotheses about derivation. Furthermore the logic needed for more accurate generalizations should be an important additional outgrowth of Huxley's article. (In the lines above which are marked with an asterisk, you should have discovered *capere* in *perceive*, *graphein* in *graphic*, and *logos* in *logic*.) Now go ahead with this review exercise. You will find help for the first two.

All Men Are Scientists

Thomas Henry Huxley

*. . . So much, then, by way of proof that the method of establishing laws in science is exactly the same as that pursued in common life. Let us now turn to another matter (though really it is but another phase of the same question), and *that is, the method by which, from the relations of certain phenomena, we prove that some stand in the position of causes towards the others.

I want to put the case clearly before you, and I will therefore show you what I mean by another familiar ___ample.

*(*establish comes* from *stabilis*, stable; a look at *stable* takes you from *stabilis* back to *stare*)

*(*relation* contains the less common form of *ferre*. See how the dictionary makes that clear.)

under, back, again

before
against
through
to/into

to/into
in

out
out

against

into

together
to or toward

back, again

before/out
for

before

not

together

against
in
to/before

*I will ___pose that one of you, on coming down in the morning to the parlour of your house, finds that a tea-pot and some spoons which had been left in the room on the ___vious evening are gone,—the window is open, and you ___serve the mark of a dirty hand on the window-frame, and ___haps, in ___dition to that, you notice the ___press of a hob-nailed shoe on the gravel outside. All these phenomena have struck your *___tention ___stantly, and before two seconds have passed you say, "Oh, somebody has broken open the window, ___tered the room, and run off with the spoons and the tea-pot!" That speech is out of your mouth in a moment. And you will probably add, "I know there has; I am quite sure of it!" You mean to say ___actly what you know; but in reality you are giving ___pression to what is, in all essential particulars, an hypothesis. You do not *know* it at all; it is nothing but an hypothesis rapidly framed in your own mind. And it is an *hypothesis founded on a long train of inductions and deductions.

What are those inductions and deductions, and how have you got at this hypothesis? You have ___served, in the first place, that the window is open; but by a train of reasoning ___volving many inductions and deductions, you have probably arrived long before at the general law—and a very good one it is—that windows do not open of themselves; and you therefore ___clude that something has opened the window. A second general law that you have ___rived at in the same way is, that tea-pots and spoons do not go out of a window spontaneously, and you are satisfied that, as they are not now where you left them, they have been ___moved. In the third place, you look at the marks on the window-sill, and the shoe-marks outside, and you say that in all ___vious ___perience the former kind of mark has never been ___duced by anything else but the hand of a human being; and the same experience shows that no other animal but man at ___sent wears shoes with hob-nails in them such as would produce the marks in the gravel. I do not know, even if we could ___cover any of those "missing links" that are talked about, that they would help us to any other ___clusion! At any rate the law which states our present experience is strong enough for my present *purpose. You next reach the conclusion, that as these kinds of marks have not been left by any other animals than men, or are liable to be formed in any other way than by a man's hand and shoe, the marks in question have been formed by a man in that way. You have, further, a general law, founded on ___servation and experience, and that, too, is, I am sorry to say, a very universal and ___peachable one,—that some men *are thieves; and you ___sume at once from all these ___mises—

and that is what __stitutes your hypothesis — that the man who made the marks outside and on the window-sill, opened the window, got into the room, and stole your tea-pot and spoons. You have now arrived at a *vera causa;* — you have

* __sumed a cause which, it is plain, is __petent to produce all the phenomena you have __served. You can __plain all these phenomena only by the hypothesis of a thief. But that is a hypothetical conclusion, of the justice of which you have no __solute proof at all; it is only rendered highly __bable by a series of inductive and deductive reasonings.

I suppose your first action, __suming that you are a man of ordinary common sense, and that you have established this hypothesis to your own satisfaction, will very likely be to go for the police, and set them on the track of the burglar, with the view to the __covery of your property. But just as you are starting with this __ject, some person comes in, and on learning what you are about, says, "My good friend, you are going on a great deal too fast. How do you know that the man who really made the marks took the spoons? It might have been a monkey that took them, and the man may have

*merely looked in afterwards." You would probably __ply, "Well, that is all very well, but you see it is contrary to all experience of the way tea-pots and spoons are __stracted; so that, at any rate, your hypothesis is less probable than mine." While you are talking the thing over in this way, another friend __rives. And he might say, "Oh, my dear sir, you are certainly going on a great deal too fast. You are most __sump-

*tous. You __mit that all these __currences took place when you were fast asleep, at a time when you could not possibly have known anything about what was taking place. How do you know that the laws of nature are not__pended during the night? It may be that there has been some kind of supernatural

* __ference in this case." In point of fact, he __clares that your hypothesis is one of which you cannot at all __monstrate the truth and that you are by no means sure that the laws of Nature are the same when you are asleep as when you are awake.

Well, now, you cannot at the moment answer that kind of reasoning. You feel that your worthy friend has you some-

*what at a __vantage. You will feel __fectly __vinced in your own mind, however, that you are quite right, and you say to him, "My good friend, I can only be guided by the natural __babilities of the case, and if you will be kind enough to stand aside and __mit me to pass, I will go and fetch the police." Well, we will suppose that your journey is __cessful, and that by good luck you meet with a policeman; that __ventually the burglar is found with your property on his person, and the marks __spond to his hand and to his boots.

together

to/together
against/out

away/forward

to

back, again
against

back, again

away

to
before
to/against

under

between/down
down, away

apart/through/with

forward
through
under

out
together, with

together

away/against
to
under

found

down/in

against

in, into
apart/against

before/in
away

down
apart/in
away

to
together

in/with
forward/wrong/back
to, toward/wrong
not
back

into/to

under

down, away/to, toward
under/to, toward
down/to/under
to/distant
against/down, away
together, with

apart

---

*Probably any jury would ___sider those facts a very good ex-perimental verification of your hypothesis, touching the cause of the ___normal phenomena ___served in your parlour, and would act ___cordingly.

*   Now, in this ___positive case, I have taken phenom-ena of a very common kind, in order that you might see what *are the different steps in an ordinary ___cess of reasoning, if you will only take the trouble to analyze it carefully, All the *operations I have ___scribed, you will see, are ___volved in the mind of any man of sense in leading him to a conclusion as to the course he should take in order to make good a robbery and punish the ___fender. I say that you are led, in that case, to your conclusion by exactly the same train of reasoning as that which a man of science pursues when he is ___deavouring to ___cover the origin and laws of the most ___cult phenom-ena. The process is, and always must be, the same; and *___cisely the same mode of reasoning was ___ployed by New-ton and Laplace in their endeavours to discover and ___fine the causes of the movements of the heavenly bodies, as you, with your own common sense, would employ to ___tect a burglar. The only ___ference is, that the nature of the ___quiry being more ___struse, every step has to be most carefully watched, so that there may not be a single crack or flaw in your hypothesis. A flaw or crack in many of the hypotheses of *daily life may be of little or no moment as ___fecting the gen-eral ___rectness of the conclusions at which we may arrive; but, in a scientific inquiry, a fallacy, great or small, is always *of ___portance, and is sure to be in the long run ___stantly ___ductive of ___chievous, if not fatal ___sults.

    Do not ___low yourselves to be ___led by the common notion that an hypothesis is ___trustworthy simply because it *is an hypothesis. It is often urged, in ___spect to some scien-tific conclusion, that, after all, it is only an hypothesis. But what more have we to guide us in nine-tenths of the most *___portant ___fairs of daily life than hypotheses, and often very ill-based ones? So that in science, where the evidence of any hypothesis is ___jected to the most rigid examination, we may rightly pursue the same course. You may have hypotheses and hypotheses. A man may say, if he likes, that the moon is made of green cheese: that is an hypothesis. But another man, who *has ___voted a great deal of time and ___tention to the ___ject, and ___vailed himself of the most powerful ___scopes and the results of the ___servations of others, ___clares that in his *opinion it is probably ___posed of materials very similar to those of which our own earth is made up: and that is also only an hypothesis. But I need not tell you that there is an enor-mous ___ference in the value of the two hypotheses. That one

which is based on sound scientific knowledge is sure to have
a ___responding value; and that which is a mere hasty random   together
guess is likely to have but little value. Every great step in our
___gress in ___covering causes has been made in exactly the   forward/apart
same way as that which I have ___tailed to you. A person   down, away
*___serving the ___currences of certain facts and phenomena   against/against
asks, naturally enough, what process, what kind of operation
*known to ___cur in Nature ___plied to the particular case, will   against/to
___ravel and ___plain the mystery? Hence you have the scien-   not/out
tific hypothesis and its value will be ___portionate to the care   for
and ___pleteness with which its basis has been tested and   together
*verified. It is in these matters as in the commonest ___fairs of   to
practical life: the guess of the fool will be folly, while the
*guess of the wise man will ___tain wisdom. In all cases, you   with
see that the value of the ___sult ___pends on the patience and   back, again/down, away
*faithfulness with which the ___vestigator ___plies to his   into/to
hypothesis every kind of verification. . . .

By this time in your word study, your various hypotheses about prefix
and root elements should demonstrate strongly "the guess of the wise."

PART FOUR

SUFFIXES

By now you know some remarkably useful prefix and root short-cuts. Are there others? Certainly. There's still one remaining shortcut, one other type of word part — the suffix — waiting to speed additional vocabulary growth.

Take the word *confer*. You can see it comes from *com-*, meaning "together," and *ferre*, meaning "to bear or carry." When you confer with someone, in a sense you "carry" yourself and your ideas to that other person. The two of you get "together."

But that's no place to stop. Look at what suffixes can add to that prefix-root combination: *conferee, conference, conferment, conferral, conferrable, conferer*, and *conferential* — not to mention *conferring, conferred*, and *confers*. With suffixes as with the other two types of word parts, when you learn one you actually learn many.

Add the suffix *-ee* to *confer* and you get *conferee*. The suffix *-ee* means "one who." That means you also know that an employee is one who is employed; a standee, one who stands; a referee, one who is referred to for crucial decisions; and an addressee, one who is addressed. And on you go.

As another example, think of the thousands of words ending in *-able* or *-ible*. When you manage one well, you have the key for managing them all. They're all manageable — learnable, memorizable, graspable. And in the process of word mastery, you become quite knowledgeable. Furthermore, subject matter, words, and word parts all become more understandable.

Do the following exercise to continue your exploration of suffix functions. Note the meaning of each suffix and the additional word clues within parentheses. Then enter the word which combines the clues in the blank at the right.

Suffixes	Meanings	Words with Suffixes
1. *-able*	Capable or worthy of the expressed or implied verb action (as with the verb *read*)	_____
2. *-er*	one who or something that performs the action indicated by the root (as with *sing*)	_____
3. *-al*	pertinence to or connection with (as *deny*)	_____
4. *-let*	smallness (as a small *pig*)	_____
5. *-tion*	an action or process (as of *defining*)	_____
6. *-ous*	full of (as with *joy*)	_____
7. *-ful*	full of (as with *hope*)	_____
8. *-ess*	a female (as a female *god*)	_____
9. *-ile*	relationship with, similarity to (*servant*)	_____
10. *-hood*	state, condition, or quality of being (child)	_____
11. *-ness*	state of (as of being *happy*)	_____
12. *-dom*	condition or state (of being *free*)	_____
13. *-ish*	resembling (a *girl*)	_____
14. *-less*	without (as without *pity*)	_____
15. *-ward*	in the direction of (the *wind*)	_____
16. *-ling*	a diminutive (as a small *duck*)	_____
17. *-ory*	having the nature of (an *illusion*)	_____
18. *-ive*	having the nature of (*destruction*)	_____
19. *-ster*	one who (belongs to a *gang*)	_____
20. *-ment*	state, quality, act of (*punishing*)	_____

Succinctness Through Suffixes

Suffixes are particularly useful in letting you express an idea with admirable conciseness, as in the examples given below. For each of the phrases, use a suffix to say the same thing with one word only.

1. If something is like silk, it is silk__.   *-y*

2. The state of being wise is what is called wis____.   *-dom*

3. Of or pertaining to an infant is infant____.   *-ile*

4. Full of or characterized by fraud is fraud_____.   *-ulent*

5. One who is young is youth___.   *-ful*

6. A Baptist believes in bapt___.   *-ism*

7. If it can be retracted, it's retract_____.   *-able*

8. If someone works without tiring, he is tire_____.   *-less*

9. If something affords remedy, it's remedi__.   *-al*

10. If it is like a picture, it's picture_____.   *-esque*

11. One who helps is a help__.   *-er*

12. If you show affection, you're affection___.   *-ate*

13. A female lion is a lion___.   *-ess*

14. Someone resembling a child is child___.   *-ish*

15. A minute globe is a glob___.   *-ule*

16. If it's worth commendation, it's commendat___.   *-ory*

17. The act of instigating a move is an instiga_____.   *-tion*

18. A scheme full of grandeur is grandi___.   *-ose*

19. Action tending toward a conclusion is conclus___.   *-ive*

20. An object moving toward heaven is going in a heaven__ direction.   *-ly*

Changing Parts of Speech

Using the appropriate suffixes, turn the following words into adjectives. Try to avoid using any *-ing* or *-ed* endings. Cover the answers in the margin with a three-by-five-inch card and go through the list as rapidly as possible.

1. advise
   advisable (or advisory)
2. earth
   earthen (or earthly)
3. glory
   glorious
4. please
   pleasant (or pleasing)
5. quarrel
   quarrelsome (or quarreling)
6. mess
   messy (or messed)
7. tiger
   tigerlike (or tigerish)
8. profit
   profitable
9. nation
   national
10. erupt
    eruptive (or erupting)

Turn the following words into verbs, through the addition of appropriate suffixes. For example, turn *glad* into *gladden* with an *-en* and the corresponding change of spelling.

1. active
   activate
2. soft
   soften
3. sterile
   sterilize
4. solid
   solidify

5. coalescence

        coalesce

6. example

        exemplify

7. refrigerator

        refrigerate

8. dark

        darken

9. machine

        mechanize

10. strength

        strengthen

Turn the following words into agent nouns—someone or something acting or doing something. For example, you could turn piano into someone playing the piano by adding *-ist*.

1. assess

        assessor

2. music

        musician

3. motor

        motorist

4. engine

        engineer

5. intoxicate

        intoxicant

6. poem

        poet

7. brag

        braggart or bragger

8. spin

        spinner or spinster

9. cool

        cooler

10. employ

        employee or employer

Turn the following words into abstract nouns, words meaning a state, act, or condition. For example, turn *apply* into *application*.

1. advertise

        advertisement

2. depart

        departure

3. sweet

        sweetness

4. loyal

   loyalty

5. man

   manhood

6. baptize

   baptism

7. admit

   admission

8. approve

   approval

9. brave

   bravery

10. jealous

    jealousy or jealousness

Suffix Mini-Review

Follow the same procedure as you have with the preceding mini-reviews, again using your three-by-five-inch card to cover the answers until you have had time to supply them. Then check immediately to correct any mistake.

Suffix	Suggested Mnemonic	Common Meaning
1. *-able, -ible*	readable	capable or worthy of
2. *-er*	singer	one who
3. *-al*	denial	pertaining to
4. *-let*	piglet	diminutive
5. *-tion, -sion, -ion*	definition	act of, process of
6. *-ous, -ose*	joyous	full of, involving
7. *-ful*	hopeful	full of
8. *-ess*	goddess	female
9. *-ile*	servile	subject to, similar to
10. *-hood*	childhood	state, condition, or quality of
11. *-ness*	happiness	state of being
12. *-dom*	freedom	state of being
13. *-ish*	childish	like or inclined to
14. *-less*	pitiless	without, unable to
15. *-ward*	windward	in the direction of
16. *-ling*	duckling	diminutive
17. *-ory*	illusory	serving to, tending to be
18. *-ive*	destructive	having the nature
19. *-ster*	gangster	one who
20. *-ment*	punishment	state, quality, or act of

PART FIVE

DICTIONARY—
Consolidating and Extending
Your Gains

Consolidating Your Gains

At this point, your best move is to go back to the initial CPD Diagnostic Test (pages 4–21). Cover your first set of answers and retake the entire test. Then compare your two sets of results to see exactly what gains you have made in each part. From that comparison you will discover two things: (1) what areas, if any, still need further study; and (2) in what area gains are sufficiently high to let you think in terms of consolidating them. After all, if you are 10 to 20 percent better, you don't want to lose those gains by failing to consolidate them.

The best way to do this is to move from theory into practice—from this vocabulary text into life, the real world of words with its letters, newspapers, magazines, and books. This payoff is crucial.

To speed you in that direction, do the next review exercise, which is structured around an actual news story. Find all examples of prefixes and root elements studied and enter them in the appropriate blanks to the left or right of the line where they appear. The blanks under each heading in the margins—*Prefixes* and *Roots*—indicate the number of elements present in the line. For example, two blanks under *Prefixes* would mean two prefixes from the twenty studied are in that line. Enter the common form of the prefix. That's the form found in the listing on page 142—not *an*, as in *annex*, but *ad-*, the common form. Enter the infinitive verb form of the roots, as in the listing on page 222. Answers are given below each passage.

Prefixes   **Roots**

1. _____

2. _____

3. _____   4. _____

5. _____   6. _____

7. _____   8. _____

9. _____

10. _____   11. _____

12. _____

13. _____

14. _____   15. _____

16. _____   17. _____

TCRT Announces 20-Cent
Cash Rate for Commuters

The fare for inter-city commuters to the university under the TCRT reduced fare experiment will be 20 cents cash or one token plus two cents cash, Luther Bakken, company general superintendent of city bus transportation, said yesterday.

Last week TCRT released information that the single fare would be 20 cents. Bakken said this move had not been approved at the time by the state railroad and warehouse commission.

The commission last week approved the special fare, but did not say what the fare would be. Bakken expects the commission to set the fare at 20 cents cash next week.

1. _____

2. _____

3. _____

4. _____

5. _____

6. _____

7. _____

Answers: PREFIXES — 1. *ad-*, 2. *com-*, 3. *inter-*, 4. *com-*, 5. *re-*, 6. *ex-*, 7. *com-*, 8. *in-*, 9. *trans-*, 10. *re-*, 11. *in-*, 12. *ad-*, 13. *com-*, 14. *com-*, 15. *ad-*, 16. *ex-*, 17. *com-*.

ROOTS: 1. *ducere*, 2. *tendere*, 3. *stare*, 4. *mittere*, 5. *mittere*, 6. *specere*, 7. *mittere*.

Here's another short article taken from the same source. Do it as you did the previous one.

Prefixes   **Roots**

1. _____   1. _____

2. _____

3. _____   4. _____   2. _____

5. _____   3. _____

6. _____

7. _____   8. _____

9. _____

10. _____   11. _____   4. _____

12. _____   13. _____   5. _____

14. _____   15. _____   6. _____

16. _____   17. _____   7. _____

18. _____   19. _____   8. _____

20. _____   21. _____   9. _____

22. _____

Union Proposals to go
to Congress Cabinet

Proposed plans for improvement of facilities in the union will be released Tuesday to the president's cabinet of all-university congress. It will then be reviewed by all student organizations on campus and eventually by the senate committee on student affairs.

The proposal, result of an extensive survey made by a university committee under the chairmanship of Dr. Taplow, associate professor of sociology, deals mainly with rearrangement of the union ground floor to better accomodate the commuters' lunchroom.

23. _____ 24. _____   The report suggested moving the lunchroom from the basement to the space

25. _____   now occupied by the union book store and

26. _____   post office, leaving only general delivery   **10.** _____

27. _____   mail service and completely dropping the post-office box system of campus mail.   **11.** _____

28. _____   Starting with the premise that (1) "the   **12.** _____

29. _____   commuters' lunchroom is horrible and (2) that something has to be done about it," the

30. _____ 31. _____   committee presented this proposal as their   **13.** _____

32. _____ 33. _____   solution to the problem.   **14.** _____

34. _____ 35. _____   However, the proposal is not offered   **15.** _____

36. _____ 37. _____   as a permanent solution. It is a suggestion   **16.** _____

38. _____ 39. _____   for rearrangement of present facilities to

40. _____ 41. _____   better advantage.   **17.** _____

Answers: PREFIXES—1. *pro-,* 2. *com-,* 3. *pro-,* 4. *in-,* 5. *re-,* 6. *pre-,* 7. *com-,* 8. *re-,* 9. *ex-,* 10. *com-,* 11. *ad-,* 12. *pro-,* 13. *re-,* 14. *ex-,* 15. *com-,* 16. *ad-,* 17. *pro-,* 18. *re-,* 19. *ad-,* 20. *ad-,* 21. *com-,* 22. *com-,* 23. *re-,* 24. *sub-,* 25. *ob-,* 26. *de-,* 27. *com-,* 28. *pre-,* 29. *com-,* 30. *com-,* 31. *pre-,* 32. *pro-,* 33. *pro-,* 34. *pro-,* 35. *ob-,* 36. *per-,* 37. *sub-,* 38. *re-,* 39. *ad-,* 40. *pre-,* 41. *ad-.*

ROOTS: 1. *ponere,* 2. *ponere,* 3. *facere,* 4. *mittere,* 5. *facere,* 6. *ponere,* 7. *tenere,* 8. *mittere,* 9. *logos,* 10. *facere.* 11. *facere,* 12. *mittere,* 13. *mittere,* 14. *ponere,* 15. *ponere,* 16. *ferre,* 17. *facere.*

    Now you're ready for your final step into the world of words. From now on, four or five times a week, take five minutes—no more— to keep your new way of looking at words fresh and viable.

    Take something you're reading—textbook, newspaper, or magazine. See how many recognizable prefixes, roots, or suffixes you can spot in three or four minutes. Then check one of your more questionable choices by turning to the dictionary.

    This procedure fixes the CPD approach (Context-Parts-Dictionary) more firmly in mind. Suppose, for example, you're reading a psychology text and come across the word *effectors.* You've never seen that word before. What does it mean?

Context. First study *context.* "The nervous system is made up of billions of tiny cells which connect with receptors, effectors, or other nerve cells." Apparently receptors and effectors have different and perhaps opposite functions, although both connect with nerve cells.

Parts. Next study word *parts.* Use the dictionary to keep you on track. Take the prefix *ef-.* That looks like an assimilated form of the common prefix *ex-,* meaning "out." To check it, look in the dictionary.

ex-¹ (iks, igz; *also occas. for 1*, eks, egz; *for 2. always* eks) [ME. < OFr. or L., akin to Gr. *ex-, exo-* < IE. base **eghs*, out] **1.** *a prefix meaning: a)* forth, from out [*expel, exert, exempt, excoriate*] *b)* beyond [*excess*] *c)* away from, out of [*expropriate, expatriate*] *d)* thoroughly [*exterminate*] *e)* upward [*exalt*] *f)* without, not having [*exanimate*] It is assimilated to *ef-* before *f* [*efface*]; *e-* before *b, d, g, l, m, n, r,* and *v* [*educe, egress, elect, emit,* etc.]: often *ec-*, before *c* or *s* [*eccentric, ecstasy*]; and, in many words of French origin, *es-* [*escape*] **2.** [orig. < L. phrases like *ex consule, ex magistro*] *a prefix, used in hyphenated compounds, meaning* former, previous, previously [*ex*-president, *ex*-convict, *ex*-wife].
ex-² (eks) *same as* EXO-: used before a vowel.

Yes, it says "Ex-becomes *ef-* before *f.*"

And *fect* is probably a form of *facere*, meaning "to make or do." Again, consult your dictionary. You can't look up *facere* but you can run your eyes down the *fac* entries and spot one that gives you those meanings, that is if you need to check that meaning by now.

fact (fakt) *n* [L. *factum*, that which is done, deed, fact, neut. pp. of *facere*, to do, act < IE. base **dhe-*, to put, place, whence DO¹, Gr. *tithenai*, to place] **1.** a deed; act: now esp. in the sense of "a criminal deed" in the phrases after the fact, before the fact [an accessory *after the fact*] **2.** a thing that has actually happened or that is really true; thing that has been or is **3.** the state of things as they are;

Finally, *-or* is a suffix meaning "that which," if you remember rightly. If you don't, there's always the dictionary.

-or (ər; *occas.* ôr) **1.** [ME. *-our* < OFr. *-our, -or, eur* < L.
-or, *-ator*] *a n.-forming*
that [*inventor, objector*
a n.-forming suffix me
error]: in Brit. usage.

Now using both context and word parts, hypothesize about the meaning of *effector*. It's not the same as a receptor, judging from context. Literally, an *effector* is "that which makes or does out." You formulate a possible definition—an effector takes nerve impulses and turns them into physical action—a making or doing which grows out of an impulse from a nerve cell.

Dictionary. Finally, check your definition in the dictionary. What does it say?

ef·fec·tor (-tər) *n.* [L., a producer < *effectus:* see EFFECT] **1.** a muscle, gland, etc. capable of responding to a stimulus, esp. to a nerve impulse **2.** that part of a nerve which transmits an impulse to an organ of response.

But there's incomplete derivational information there. For more you have to look back at part of the entry for *effect* to make sure your analysis was accurate. Here's that information:

ef·fect (e fekt', i-) *n.* [ME. < OFr. (& L.) < L. *effectus.* orig., pp. of *efficere,* to bring to pass, accomplish < *ex-.* out + *facere,* DO¹] **1.** anything brought about by a cause or agent; result **2.** the power or ability to bring about

You may say, "Why go to all that work when you can just look up *effector* and be done with it?" When you do that, you know only one thing—the meaning of *effector*. When you use the approach here, you learn *many* things with one look. Your glance at one entry—the entry for *ex-*, for example—helps you understand better such other difficult words as *effable, efface, efferent, effervesce, effete, efficacy, effigy, effloresce, effulgent, effuse,* and *effusive.* Linking all such words with *ex-* and the idea of "out" makes them easier to define as well as to remember.

So much for an illustration of how you consolidate efforts with the CPD approach, word elements, and your good friend the dictionary. Choosing words in this way, three or four a week, insures the strongest possible focus on words of prime importance to you. After all, you select them from material met in your own normal reading and listening.

That's how you consolidate your gains. Certainly five minutes a day, four or five times a week, is a small price to pay for keeping the gains you've made.

Extending Your Gains with the LDE Formula

Consolidating is important but even more important is extending your gains. And with the background you have built and the momentum you have developed, extending your gains can be done with almost as little effort as consolidating them—just a few minutes a week.

What you need is a way to facilitate your attack on any and all unknown words—a way to speed the generalization process. This will let you go far beyond the few elements you have already studied, important though they are. The LDE formula is designed to meet that very need. It lets you harness brain power to word power—an unbeatable combination. You see, what's in your head is far more important than what's in your dictionary. Furthermore, you always have your head with you. You don't always have your dictionary.

How does the LDE formula work? In class when a student is asked what the Latin word *omnis* means, a blank look and a "don't know" are the usual responses. The student may add, "I never had any Latin."

With the LDE formula you never need to say, "I don't know." You start thinking in a certain pattern first. For example, you actually do know what *omnis* means, and what hundreds of other Latin and Greek words mean. You just don't know you know. That's where the LDE formula comes in.

L stands for *list*, your first step. List as many words as you can, beginning with the same combination of letters found in the unknown word, in this case, beginning with *omni*. Perhaps you think of *omnidirectional* and *omnipotent*. Maybe that's all you can think of, offhand. Or you may list more—*omnipresent, omnivorous,* and *omniscient*. You don't always need that many, although usually the more the better. Sometimes only one, such as *omnidirectional*, is enough. That's step one—*list*.

Next, *define* as many of the listed words as you can. You may define *omnidirectional*, for example, as "in all directions," and *omnipotent* as "all-powerful."

Your third and last step is to *extract* the common denominator of meaning from the listed words. After all, if the words have a part in common they should also have a meaning in common, the one contributing to the other. In the definitions—"in all directions" and "all-powerful"—the common denominator of meaning is *all*. Thus, you really do know what *omnis* means, even though you thought you didn't. Just *list*, *define*, *extract*; use the LDE formula.

Take another example. What does the Latin word *gress* mean? List some *gress* words. Here you have to add prefixes to make your list. Perhaps you list *progress*. Think of some other prefixes and add them to make *regress, transgress,* and *digress*.

Now define each. If you make progress, you "go forward." If you *regress*, you "go back or backwards." If you *transgress*, you "go beyond" usual bounds in your behavior. Finally, if you *digress*, you "go away or apart" from your subject.

Your last step, to extract the common denominator of meaning, should be easy: it's "go."

From now on use that formula with strange words and word parts. The more you use it, the easier it becomes. If you have trouble sometimes extracting the common meaning, just remember that even if it works only a low 60 percent of the time, it's still worth using. It gives you a 60 percent advantage over those who don't know it or don't use it. That's still an advantage very much worth having. Furthermore, every time you learn a single new element, you have actually learned many. *Omni,* for example, comes over into English in so few words—only about twenty—that it is not the best of shortcuts. Yet even with it, you have increased your vocabulary by a leap of twenty when you understand its meaning.

Extending Your Prefix Knowledge

You have already studied the most important prefixes. Extend your acquaintance to the twenty prefixes next in importance, prefixes providing shortcuts to over 2,000 additional words. To fit the LDE formula, one word with each prefix is given in parentheses to start your list. See how it helps you arrive at the right meaning.

1. *a-* (atypical): (1) from; (2) after; (3) not; (4) single; (5) also

    1. _____

2. *semi-* (semicircle): (1) small; (2) twice; (3) half; (4) before; (5) party

    2. _____

3. *fore-* (foremost): (1) more; (2) see; (3) less; (4) before; (5) up

    3. _____

4. *super-* (superman): (1) below; (2) great; (3) small; (4) equal; (5) above

    4. _____

5. *di-* (divide): (1) twice; (2) four; (3) against; (4) cut; (5) separate

    5. _____

6. *ana-* (analysis): (1) outside; (2) all; (3) up or back; (4) one; (5) inside

    6. _____

7. *multi-* (multistage): (1) increase; (2) add; (3) many; (4) move; (5) magnify

    7. _____

8. *eu-* (eulogy): (1) one; (2) slow; (3) on; (4) good; (5) small

    8. _____

9. *micro-* (microscope): (1) carrier; (2) small; (3) magnified; (4) round

    9. _____

10. *iso-* (isomer): (1) away; (2) upward; (3) alone; (4) equal; (5) one

    10. _____

Now try a different pattern. The next ten words contain the following prefixes: *photo-, meta-, uni-, pyro-, circum-, electro-, bio-, cata-, counter-,* and *post-.* Put the LDE formula to work in getting prefix meaning and then in getting word meaning.

Word to be defined	Prefix	Prefix meaning	Probable meaning of word to be defined	
1. photogene	_____	_____	(1) body cell; (2) germ; (3) afterimage; (4) nerve ending	1. _____
2. metaphrase	_____	_____	(1) grow sick; (2) translate; (3) combine; (4) disappear	2. _____
3. unipod	_____	_____	(1) seed; (2) tendril; (3) sure footed; (4) one legged	3. _____
4. pyretic	_____	_____	(1) feverish; (2) toothy; (3) nervous; (4) tasteless	4. _____
5. circumlocution	_____	_____	(1) slogan; (2) roundabout way of speaking (3) around the corner; (4) contradiction	5. _____
6. electron	_____	_____	(1) molecule; (2) negatively charged particle; (3) radio; (4) current	6. _____
7. biotic	_____	_____	(1) of life; (2) scientific; (3) medicine; (4) changing	7. _____
8. catafalque	_____	_____	(1) storeroom; (2) long corridor; (3) funeral canopy; (4) opening	8. _____

9. countermand _____ _____ (1) false money; (2) to store; (3) aim; (4) revoke 9. _____

10. postprandial _____ _____ (1) progressive; (2) firmly fixed; (3) after dinner; (4) practical 10. _____

(Answers on page 260.)

Extending Your Root Knowledge

Do the same thing with the following twenty roots of next importance as you did with the preceding twenty prefixes.

1. *regere* (regulate): (1) rule; (2) sign; (3) entertain; (4) regret; (5) shelter 1. _____

2. *videre* (video): (1) eat; (2) catch; (3) value; (4) see; (5) shake 2. _____

3. *cedere* (concede): (1) halt; (2) raise; (3) withdraw; (4) plant; (5) make 3. _____

4. *movere* (remove): (1) mourn; (2) move; (3) place; (4) rise; (5) draw 4. _____

5. *legere* (legend): (1) travel; (2) gather; (3) lecture; (4) teach; (5) guide 5. _____

6. *trahere* (tractor): (1) run; (2) trade; (3) draw; (4) change; (5) pay 6. _____

7. *agere* (agent): (1) inquire; (2) repeat; (3) terrify; (4) agitate; (5) act 7. _____

8. *venire* (advent): (1) come; (2) revenge; (3) circulate; (4) praise; (5) age 8. _____

9. *vertere* (revert): (1) speak; (2) inform; (3) turn; (4) watch; (5) travel 9. _____

10. *portare* (porter):   (1) open; (2) practice; (3) prepare;
     (4) carry; (5) work   10. _____

Now try the other pattern. Look for a strange root in each of the following words. Put the LDE formula to work in getting its probable meaning. Then use that knowledge to get the word meaning.

Word to be defined	Root	Root meaning	Probable meaning of word to be defined	
1. *sequacious*	_____	_____	(1) talkative; (2) inclined to follow; (3) persistent; (4) able to fight	1. _____
2. *seclusive*	_____	_____	(1) closed off; (2) second rate; (3) cluttered; (4) timbered	2. _____
3. *format*	_____	_____	(1) formality; (2) foreign office; (3) principle; (4) makeup	3. _____
4. *vivace*	_____	_____	(1) soft; (2) musical; (3) lively; (4) vocal; (5) brassy	4. _____
5. *cursory*	_____	_____	(1) rapid; (2) careful; (3) harsh; (4) medical	5. _____
6. *sentient*	_____	_____	(1) waiting; (2) conscious; (3) separate; (4) hidden	6. _____
7. *sedentary*	_____	_____	(1) treasonable; (2) helpful; (3) thick; (4) sitting	7. _____
8. *construe*	_____	_____	(1) attack; (2) win; (3) plan; (4) explain	8. _____
9. *pendulous*	_____	_____	(1) turning; (2) swinging; (3) entering; (4) repeating	9. _____
10. *stricture*	_____	_____	(1) struggle; (2) limitation; (3) rope; (4) compliment	10. _____

Alphabetical listing of roots: *claudere, currere, forma, pendere, sedere, sentire, sequi, stringere, struere, vivere. (Answers on page 269.)*

Don't be discouraged if you got only 50 percent of these difficult test items right. Just remember, that's probably 50 percent *better* than someone else who doesn't know or use the LDE formula.

Extending Beyond English

Do you appreciate to the full the value of your newly gained insights? Do you realize how useful the *Fourteen Words That Make All the Difference* really are? To find out, try the following test. It's not even a test of English words. It's a French vocabulary test. But the elements you have studied are present, not only in English, but in *all* romance languages. This is the acid test of your ability to use the derivational approach set forth in this text.

Deduce the meaning of each of the following French words. Look for familiar prefix and root elements. If you deduce accurately, you should have close to a perfect score with these strangest of words. Try the test, then lean back with satisfaction. You will realize how much you have progressed in developing top-level skill in dealing with words.

1. *tenu:*   (1) sore; (2) kept; (3) hard; (4) long; (5) sent   1. _____

2. *capter:*   (1) fly; (2) tip over; (3) collect; (4) throw; (5) stagger   2. _____

3. *detruire:*   (1) trust; (2) pull down; (3) put up; (4) move; (5) get   3. _____

4. *interrompre:*   (1) break in; (2) trample; (3) attempt; (4) enter   4. _____

5. *fait:*   (1) frame; (2) failure; (3) hope; (4) deed; (5) flaw   5. _____

6. *plisser:*   (1) help; (2) sharpen; (3) grasp; (4) pleat; (5) pledge   6. _____

7. *souscrire:*   (1) frighten; (2) underwrite; (3) shout; (4) entertain   7. _____

8. *extraire:*   (1) heat up; (2) pull out; (3) fill up; (4) turn over

8. _____

9. *demunir:*   (1) build; (2) part with; (3) raise; (4) move in; (5) run

9. _____

10. *pliage:*   (1) plunge; (2) smooth; (3) creasing; (4) pleasing

10. _____

11. *stationnaire:*   (1) starter; (2) standard; (3) questionnaire; (4) fixed

11. _____

12. *invoquer:*   (1) mock; (2) invent; (3) invoke; (4) help; (5) turn

12. _____

13. *obtenir:*   (1) donate; (2) get; (3) advertise; (4) open; (5) harm

13. _____

14. *captage:*   (1) flying; (2) dropping; (3) picking up; (4) putting on

14. _____

15. *colloque:*   (1) hearing; (2) conversation; (3) puzzle; (4) lock

15. _____

16. *preavis:*   (1) view; (2) extension; (3) food; (4) forewarning

16. _____

17. *proscrire:*   (1) praise; (2) shake; (3) prohibit; (4) suffer; (5) leave

17. _____

18. *insoumis:*   (1) unruly; (2) witty; (3) soft; (4) sleepy; (5) sunny

18. _____

19. *debrouiller:*   (1) trust; (2) disentangle; (3) build; (4) accelerate

19. _____

20. *compatir:*   (1) speak; (2) strike; (3) run; (4) sympathize; (5) strain

20. _____

(*Answers on page 261.*)

What's Next?

You've made real progress in improving your vocabulary. What do you do next? Why not keep all the momentum you've established by using one of the following new and totally different aids?

1. Add an important visual dimension to your vocabulary-building efforts. Telstar Productions, Inc. (366 North Prior, St. Paul, Minnesota 55104) has produced a series of twelve videotaped lessons in color for use in learning centers or language laboratories. The lessons vary in length from five to eleven minutes and provide dramatic treatment of context and word parts to accelerate further learning. Inquire at your nearest university or college to see if they are available for your use.

2. Use the *Word Power Game,* available from Telstar ($5.00 postpaid). It is a deck of seventy-two cards, color-coded to heighten your awareness of prefixes, roots, and suffixes. Directions are given for playing several games, including a vocabulary-building game of solitaire. A card-a-day plan is also described. In a study involving 598 students, the best gains were achieved through use of these cards—3.37 percent improvement for each hour spent in use. The deck contains not fourteen but thirty-two root cards, plus two jokers with thirty-six additional Latin and Greek prefixes and roots. Word parts tend to be almost invisible until you start using these cards. For example, one root card with the Latin verb *videre* can be used together with twenty other cards in the deck to make over fifty different words. Try listing fifty words containing *vid* yourself without the help of the cards and you can see the advantage of this game.

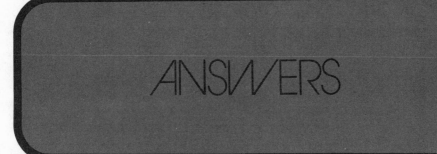

ANSWERS

CPD diagnostic tests

I Context		II Parts			III Dictionary
	TestA:	*Test B:*	*Test C:*	*Test D:*	
1. 3	1. 3	1. 4	1. 1	1. 5	1. 2
2. 4	2. 4	2. 3	2. 4	2. 5	2. 6
3. 1	3. 4	3. 4	3. 5	3. 4	3. — (irony)
4. 2	4. 1	4. 4	4. 4	4. 1	4. 1
5. 2	5. 4	5. 1	5. 1	5. 1	5. 3
6. 4	6. 3	6. 5	6. 5	6. 2	6. 1
7. 3	7. 2	7. 4	7. 3	7. 5	7. to, at, toward
8. 1	8. 4	8. 1	8. 4	8. 1	8. yes
9. 4	9. 4	9. 2	9. 2	9. 2	9. yes
10. 2	10. 5	10. 3	10. 2	10. 5	10. astringent
	11. 1	11. 5	11. 1	11. 3	11. alleviate
	12. 5	12. 1	12. 4	12. 5	12. Latin
	13. 1	13. 5	13. 5	13. 3	13. Middle English
	14. 3	14. 2	14. 1	14. 1	14. to behold
	15. 4	15. 2	15. 2	15. 2	15. spectacle

16. 1	16. 2	16. 4	16. 4	16. appearance, apparition
17. 1	17. 1	17. 2	17. 2	17. to know
18. 1	18. 4	18. 2	18. 1	18. word and suffix
19. 3	19. 1	19. 2	19. 4	19. 2
20. 5	20. 4	20. 3	20. 1	20. bashfulness

Opposites Review Test (page 38)

1. 2	6. 4
2. 4	7. 2
3. 1	8. 2
4. 3	9. 1
5. 2	10. 2

De — Review Test (page 51)

1. 4
2. 2
3. 3
4. 2
5. 1

Verbal Analogy Review Test (page 51)

1. heat before	6. inflate
2. ending	7. frost
3. fore	8. accelerate
4. lude	9. pre-
5. down, away	10. remove

Review Test I: (page 60)

A	B	C
1. 7	1. 1	1. 2
2. 5	2. 4	2. 4
3. 8	3. 3	3. 2
4. 2	4. 2	4. 4
5. 6	5. 1	5. 1

Contextual Clues (page 62)

1. 3
2. 5
3. 2
4. 5
5. 3

Re—Review Test (page 71)

1. 2
2. 1
3. 4
4. 1
5. 1

Verbal Analogy Review Test (page 84)

1. back
2. non
3. pro
4. de
5. across

Review Test II (page 85)

A	B	C
1. 5	1. 2	1. noncollegiate
2. 2	2. 2	2. progress
3. 7	3. 4	3. transatlantic
4. 1	4. 3	4. unexpected
5. 5	5. 3	5. recalls

Review Test III (page 113)

A	B	C
1. 6	1. 4	1. 2
2. 4	2. 2	2. 4
3. 7	3. 2	3. 1
4. 3	4. 4	4. 3
5. 1	5. 5	5. 1

Sentence Completion Test (page 114)

1. 3	6. 1
2. 1	7. 5
3. 2	8. 3
4. 3	9. 5
5. 5	10. 1

Opposites Review Test (page 138)

1. 3	6. 2	11. 3	16. 3
2. 4	7. 2	12. 3	17. 2
3. 2	8. 4	13. 3	18. 4
4. 1	9. 4	14. 1	19. 3
5. 3	10. 1	15. 3	20. 4

Review Test IV (page 141)

A	B	C
1. 2 or 6	1. 1	1. *in*gress
2. 4	2. 2	2. *e*gress
3. 5	3. 6	3. *agg*ressively
4. 2 or 6	4. 3	4. *con*gress
5. 7	5. 4	5. *re*gressing
		*pro*gressing

Capere Review Exercise (page 155)

1. capacity
2. principal
3. Emancipate
4. precepts
5. Perceive
6. Accept
7. capable
8. anticipating
9. exceptions
10. occupy

Ponere Review Exercise (page 160)

1. positive
2. position
3. compose
4. postpone
5. disposition
6. postage
7. deposit
8. depository
9. supposition
10. post

Tenere Review Exercise (page 164)

1. content
2. tenaciously
3. pertaining
4. retain
5. obtain
6. continue
7. sustain
8. maintain
9. continual
10. entertaining

Ducere Review Exercise (page 168)

1. conduct	6. productive
2. reduce	7. deductions
3. produce	8. educe
4. educated	9. productiveness
5. introduced	10. conducive

Mittere Review Exercise (page 172)

1. committing	6. intermittent
2. Permit	7. transmits
3. admit	8. emit
4. omit	9. promise
5. Submit	10. dismiss

Review Test V (page 172)

A	B	C
1. 4	1. 2	1. except
2. 6	2. 1	2. deposit
3. 1	3. 4	3. retain
4. 7	4. 1	4. induct
5. 3	5. 1	5. emitting

Verbal Analogy Review Test (page 174)

1. 2	6. 1	11. 2	16. 1
2. 2	7. 1	12. 4	17. 2
3. 3	8. 3	13. 1	18. 1
4. 3	9. 4	14. 3	19. 2
5. 4	10. 2	15. 4	20. 3

Scribere Review Exercise (page 180)

1. script	6. scribe
2. scribble	7. manuscript
3. describe	8. inscription
4. prescribe	9. subscribe
5. transcribe	10. postscript

Facere Review Exercise (page 185)

1. affects	6. feature
2. fact	7. proficient
3. perfectly	8. facilitate
4. effective	9. factor
5. difficult	10. manufactures

Tendere Review Exercise (page 190)

1. tends	6. pretend
2. extend	7. intently
3. Attention	8. tendency
4. contend	9. extensive
5. intention	10. portend

Specere Review Exercise (page 195)

1. special	6. auspicious
2. perspicacity	7. inspecting
3. expect	8. expectation
4. prospect	9. specimens
5. retrospect	10. respect

Plicare Review Exercise (page 200)

1. apply	6. multiply
2. simple	7. comply
3. complex	8. explicit
4. deploy	9. implicit
5. application	10. Employ

Stare Review Exercise (page 204)

1. obstacles	6. distance
2. persist	7. instant
3. substantial	8. stationary
4. assist	9. assistance
5. desist	10. establishing

Review Test VI (page 205)

A	B	C
1. 3	1. 1	1. description
2. 6	2. 2	2. feasible
3. 8	3. 3	3. attend
4. 2	4. 4	4. inspect
5. 5	5. 2	5. implied

Ferre Review Exercise (page 210)

1. ferry	6. defer
2. Relating	7. delay
3. different	8. elation
4. preference	9. suffer
5. offered	10. proffer

Graphein Review Exercise (page 216)

1. bibliography
2. autograph
3. biographer
4. calligraphy
5. orthography
6. photographer
7. seismograph
8. lexicographer
9. stenographer
10. paragraph

Logos Review Exercise (page 220)

1. catalog
2. etymology
3. phraseology
4. theology
5. monologue
6. dialogue
7. philology
8. prologue
9. travelogue
10. terminology

Review Test VII (page 221)

A	B	C
1. 3	1. 2	1. status
2. 7	2. 1	2. inferred
3. 5	3. 4	3. autograph
4. 6	4. 2	4. dialogue

Suffixes (page 232)

1. readable
2. singer
3. denial
4. piglet
5. definition
6. joyous
7. hopeful
8. goddess
9. servile
10. childhood
11. happiness
12. freedom
13. girlish
14. pitiless
15. windward
16. duckling
17. illusory
18. destructive
19. gangster
20. punishment

Extending Your Prefix Knowledge (page 247)

1. 3	6. 3	1. 3	6. 2
2. 3	7. 3	2. 2	7. 1
3. 4	8. 4	3. 4	8. 3
4. 5	9. 2	4. 1	9. 4
5. 1	10. 4	5. 2	10. 3

Extending Your Root Knowledge (page 249)

1. 1	6. 3	1. 2	6. 2
2. 4	7. 5	2. 1	7. 4
3. 3	8. 1	3. 4	8. 4
4. 2	9. 3	4. 3	9. 2
5. 2	10. 4	5. 1	10. 2

Extending Beyond English (page 251)

1. 2	6. 4	11. 4	16. 4
2. 3	7. 2	12. 3	17. 3
3. 2	8. 2	13. 2	18. 1
4. 1	9. 2	14. 3	19. 2
5. 4	10. 3	15. 2	20. 4